WHAT REMAINS IS LOVE

55 Letters to My Mother

KIM COOK

To mothers, sisters, grandmothers—
women who have lived and learned and struggled
and loved and held each other through it all,
across generations of time.

Do you have the patience to wait
till the mud settles and the water is clear?
Can you remain unmoving
till the right action arises by itself?

The Master doesn't seek fulfillment.
Not seeking, not expecting,
she is present, and can welcome all things.

Tao te Ching
Translation by Stephen Mitchell ©1988
First HarperPerennial Edition published 1991

Contents

Preface

My mother used to say that people who have interesting lives don't have time to clean their homes. While this was, in part, a defensive explanation for what started out as a messy home and ended up as chaos, I think it was also a rebuttal and a rebuke of her former life. Born with an incredible intellect, yet later consigned to the role of housewife, she broke loose to the Berkeley of the '60s. No more keeping a tidy house for her.

Her approach to parenting was similar to her approach to housekeeping. While she tried, and she cared, her method eventually added up to a fair amount of neglect. Ultimately, she sat my sister and me down and said she could be either a good scientist or a good mother, but not both. And, she thought she had a better chance at being a good scientist, so we were sent away to separate schools.

When I weave it all together, I see that my complex relationship with my mother is the great love affair of my life, and also a great tragedy. Our estrangement at the end of her life left me feeling bereft, even though there are ways being apart from her served me. Furthermore, I had the sense from her friends and some members of our family that I, her daughter, somehow was not truly entitled to grieve.

I wrote these letters five years after my mother passed. From the time she died, I felt like there was writing inside me about our love and my loss—but not as a process of grief or recrimination. I needed to be resolved about our relationship, to work through the feelings that lingered, and then I could write. This is not to say that I had nothing left to feel, but it was after the upheaval and confusion of my initial loss that the writing came. It came when I began to notice how my mother was showing up in my everyday life. In both simple and large ways, she continued to be present in my landscape and a part of my world. I began to write. And once I started, the letters arrived on their own in a flurry of memories and topics both nostalgic and painful.

I know that people lose people they love all the time. I know that mother-daughter relationships are complex. It is also my understanding that millions of people lose family members with unresolved estrangements. It is my hope that my letters will bring comfort, or a sense of identification, or a recognition that there is beauty in love that is flawed and painful. They are an offering, a poem of sorts, a conclusion to a timeless story (or perhaps an evolution). May they serve you as they have served me in the telling as a coming home to truth and finding ourselves still whole regardless of what transpired on the journey.

Finally, I want to acknowledge that what I am writing about is not always easy to read. It is a way of breaking silence and sharing family secrets. The people in my family were, and are, whole human beings who cannot be reduced to either all-good or all-bad figures. They were wonderful, they were burdened, and they did the best they could with what they had. Furthermore, my family has always had an intense ethos about professional achievement and civic participation. It is not my desire to undermine those contributions, rather to say that sometimes, the underbelly needs to be seen. It is important that people who suffer, who have suffered, hear the voices of others who have experienced something similar and come through it. That is me. I write for you, I write for me, and most of all, I write in the name of the love I have for my mother.

Our home with plants, bells, and art.
The woman pictured is unknown.

1

—

LPs

Dear Mom,

I am missing you today. This is not unusual.

Recently the shelf that held the LPs that belonged to you collapsed in the hallway. It came straight down, and the LPs stayed upright and intact, not spilling. The books on the shelf below squished out like almond butter from a sandwich, spreading onto the floor, crowding the hallway. Two shelves pancaked with no breakage. I took the LPs from their now-collapsed shelving and leaned them along the wall. In a cautionary choice, I also took the rest of the LPs from another shelf and laid them along the wall as well. The books got stacked, and there they sat for two weeks as I acknowledged this needed addressing but did not commence the next steps.

Today, as I prepare to leave for Montreal and begin new work in a new city, I need to have as much order as I can summon. Even though I am not letting go of my apartment in the Bay Area, I need to feel surrounded by my home and experience myself taking care of me, playing house. The dishes are done, laundry is happening, and the long list of other tasks I may need to address (like packing) are being tabled while I attempt to gather myself. I sit in the hall, on the floor, to look at the books first. I may have reduced my books in last year's project to follow Marie Kondo's guidance in *The Life-Changing Magic of Tidying Up*, but it's worth looking to see if I might let go of some of what I have stacked in the hall. And yes, about half of them can go for resell at the local bookshop before the remainder find their way back on the shelf or to the donation stop on San Pablo Avenue.

Then the LPs, the records. I think I will see which ones "spark joy," and this will be a weeding-out process. Like the books. The first records are Brahms, Beethoven, Berlioz, Chopin, Cesar Franck, and Francois Couperin. Letting go is not so easy. Surely, I should listen to all of Beethoven before deciding if I can let some go. Obviously I should educate myself about Berlioz. The Brahms and the Chopin are going to be lovely. And the Couperin, well, there is something very important about the Couperin. Francois Couperin summons the past, the exact precise room in North Berkeley, with the bay windows and the hardwood floors covered by the carpet that our Uncle Phil, your brother-in-law, gave to us when he married your sister Jean. The plants placed all around and hanging in, yes, macrame holders; the roman window shades you made based on an idea you had, strung in the back with little plastic hoops, using laundry twine to raise and lower them and cup hooks to fasten them at the bottom. The stereo in the corner of the dining room, and Couperin playing while I jumped and spun and pointed my toes, imagining myself a ballerina. Well, these records must stay.

Moving on to a new section, this one with Jacques Brel; Chinese, Tibetan, and Japanese traditional music; Mexican folk songs; Ravi Shankar; and tablas recordings—a whole international treasure trove of music that evokes you, your eclectic tastes, and your passion for a sense of a world that exists far beyond our home. Clearly, I need these, too. After all, I might discover some fabulous soundtrack for a show I haven't made yet.

And then, Joni Mitchell, a recording purchased at the time it was released. We were the peace and love generation—we really would sing of paving paradise and putting up a parking lot. Any minute now, I am likely to come across Malvina Reynolds and her music of little boxes on a hillside that we would sing on our way to the airport, passing by South San Francisco where those exact little houses in pastel colors were in view. Those trips to the airport that involved leaving you to visit our father in the San Joaquin Valley, a small world far away from the expansive world of music and revolution and a freedom to explore that you were creating.

I long for you. I long for you as the one who I felt truly connected to in these creative ways. These ways of music, of peace rallies singing Country Joe McDonald songs, and of winter holidays filled with the six sides of LPs it took to play the whole Messiah by Handel. Just holding your LPs summons thoughts of you and your joy and quest for a big world. The drive that took you from your small town, your traumatic past, to the Berkeley of the '60s, with my sister Meredith and me in the back, the U-Haul truck trailing behind, and the future you forged for all of us just ahead. I offer you this memory.

I love you,
Kim

Kim Cook; photo by Kerry Kehoe.

2
—
Move Out

Dear Mom,

This morning I had a dream we were living together—you, me, and Meredith. Not in a familiar place but a lesser-known place of dreams, even a bit conventional, like a ranch home in a Florida suburb. In this dream, I was attending classes at a junior college, but more as a career interlude and not as the main priority in my life. And then, something happened between us, and you wanted me to move out. Immediately. That day. You were angry.

You felt I had misrepresented myself as knowing things I did not actually know and managing money better than I actually had. In my dream, I was to leave, now, and you and Meredith would stay. I felt so much grief at this rejection. This putting aside of me. I pushed back initially, not ready to go, and did not leave that day. I hoped you would change your mind during the night. But the next day, the force of your will to have me gone was decisive. I knew I had to find a place to live, right now. Perhaps with my best friend Joni, who was there for me at the beginning of my time in recovery from trauma, alcoholism, and addiction. The prominent features of this dream were the rejection and the grief.

I woke up this morning, and as I reflected on the dream and my recent days at my new job in Montreal, anxious about whether I was making the right impression, I recalled the many times you said I was an embarrassment to you. You specifically told me that I embarrassed you. That memory is not a dream. How deeply sad that makes me even now, lying in my bed in the after-dream haze of recall. How much I carry a sense that I am weird and doing all the wrong things. I work for a company now that says, "We do it in public" as their tagline. I wonder if today I can be my weird, dance-in-the-streets, tell-it-like-it-is, hug people, laugh-and-be-goofy self.

I am sad about the nature of our relationship and about the profound and deeply felt well of sorrow at being told to leave in the dream that is a reflection of your actual repeated requests to "go, now, I don't want you here." I feel we failed to love each other with a fierce holding on and instead the going away became the norm. I miss you.

I love you,
Kim

3

—

Black Pepper

Dear Mom,

After you died, when I made eggs, I fixated on black pepper. I put pepper on my eggs because of you. Never mind that people all over the world put pepper on their eggs. I pepper my eggs because you loved pepper on your eggs. As a little girl, I was not in favor of pepper on my eggs, but somewhere in there, I became a pepper-on-my-eggs person. It became a part of me, my habit, my world.

When we first moved to Berkeley in 1966, your life came into definition. You went forward. Fully. You read Adelle Davis's book *Let's Eat Right to Keep Fit*. You made us her breakfast drink called "Pep-Up" in pewter sherry glasses, and Meredith and I had to drink it in the morning with turned-up noses and screwed-up faces. Yuck! It's funny, you weren't really a cook, but you went full force with passion into some things, and health food became one of those things.

We went to the Food Mill in East Oakland for fresh ground almond butter, where we could see the machines in action, and we purchased "crunchy granola" before there were any granola brands to speak of. On the

Mom studying at home in Berkeley.

other end of the spectrum, you liked to make souffles, beef bourguignon, cheese fondue, and cheese blintzes. You made homemade yogurt for years, and perfected a chocolate mousse made with whipping cream instead of egg whites that filled empty jam jars and lived available for yummy consumption in our fridge.

This was not a consistent set of conditions, but it was certainly a memorable recurring event. Fun. Lively. As I write this, I feel the flurry of energy around your burst of passion for food. It sits beside memories of how you made our home function with no money.

These domestic moments are in contrast to the many nights when you were studying in the lab and not home at all. And the years when Meredith and I shopped and cooked for ourselves. It's hard to know the balance in terms of time. One side is full of light and bright, the other full of dark and sad. The proportions are unclear even though the impressions are distinct. Thank you, Mom.

I love you,

Kim

Kim at kiss kiss bear hug time on the top bunk.

4

—

Bedtime Rituals

Dear Mom,

I am thinking tonight of bedtime rituals. Somehow, it has been elusive for me to brush my teeth (much less floss) and wash my face before bed. I noticed this again this evening when I felt a small sense of self-congratulation as I recognized that I've washed my face, flossed, and brushed my teeth most of the last ten nights. Why is this a victory?

There are these ways, these lingering ways, in which the more neglectful side of my childhood shows up through time. This nightly resistance to self-care is one of those ways. I recall nights without someone to put me to bed. Nights when Meredith and I would have to leave the next-door neighbor's home, after she fed us dinner, and walk ourselves across the courtyard, into the dark house, and up the stairs to go to bed. Always nervous about the unknown at the top of the stairs, nighttime rituals related to hygiene were not of concern. Who would go up the stairs first—usually Meredith because I was bigger and somehow made her do it—took great precedence over any other aspects of bedtime.

And yet, and still, I also have memories of when you were there, of protracted nighttime rituals, including chants that went something like, "sweet dreams, don't let the bed bugs bite, kiss kiss bear hug." So much sweetness that I can feel a twinge of sorrow and longing at the recollection of those moments.

Today, I know that the small things—make the bed, eat well, exercise, go to bed early enough to get good sleep, wash my face, and yes, floss and brush my teeth—are the habits that challenge me. When I manage to do them, I recognize them as the hallmarks of progress, the small victories that mean I am somehow just a little bit better than I once was, in all the ways that count. Small things.

My heart feels heavy as I write this. We had a very confusing relationship when I was little. You gave me some loving that was passionate and inspiring, but your nurturing was erratic to nonexistent. It must have been so hard for you to have children and figure out how to take care of yourself and us. But I did wash, floss, and brush tonight, and I am claiming my victories in small things. Good night, sweet dreams, don't let the bed bugs bite, kiss kiss bear hug.

I love you, Mom.
I truly do.
Kim

5

—

Barn Jacket

Dear Mom,

Today I bought a jacket for $1,195 Canadian dollars plus tax. A pretty expensive jacket, right? Here are some of the ways I worked to rationalize it in my mind:

- Celebrating my new life in Montreal.
- It's fashionable.
- It's 25 percent less because in the US. It's the same price, but Canadian dollars are seventy-five cents to the U.S. dollar.
- It's art.

As I worked through rationalizing and purchasing the jacket and then left the store, I thought of you. In part, I thought of you because I think you might have appreciated the jacket as art. It is beautiful. And while it is called a barn jacket, it's not likely it will be worn near a barn by anyone who buys it, so it doesn't exactly pass as practical with its faux fur collar and hip-hitting length. That makes it an unlikely piece of clothing for Montreal's cold winters, but perhaps for the earlier days of winter or the later days of fall. Really, why did I buy it? It was a thing

The Barn Jacket.

of beauty and I wanted it. I imagine you could relate to that justification.

While you were mostly broke in the early part of your life, in your later years, you were able to buy many things of beauty. So, today, I bought the jacket. Afterward, as I rode the bus across Montreal, I heard a young woman on the phone defending her spending to her mother, saying, "I had to buy books, there are lots of new expenses, school is just starting." Seemingly, she is here to go to college and was calling home for more money.

I am reminded of similar conversations with you and, when I was younger, with your father. I faced the questioning of why I needed money, and being called a "bum," until the day came when the cost of asking was greater than the cost of finding out what would happen if I went through what I was going through without financial help. I would have been shamed by you—and worse, I would be tuning back into the broadcast that said I was a loser. I stood steadfast and watched my belongings go, secure in the knowledge that I was fortunate to have them to sell, and slowly, slowly I drifted even closer to the edge, to the precipice of homelessness, as I fell further and further behind on the rent. That became the beginning of my turnaround.

Today, I have some money. I can afford that crazy barn jacket purchase. Still, it rattles me. You went through an actual fortune. I have some number of thousands. I am hoping to grow old, to stay healthy, and to be able to afford my rent on some distant (I hope) day when I perhaps am no longer earning (although I hope to work and joyfully earn until the week that I lay down my burden and shuffle off this mortal coil, as they say). But

I am afraid, afraid of the rationalization, the seductive nature of spending that may have imprinted from you to me, the misuse of my own good fortune, and the echoes of remonstrations over the use of funds and any requests for help—all conflicting messages about money, shame, abundance, and lack.

I am glad you spent your money before you died. Which is not the same as saying I am glad you died. Because I am not. I am sad about that. Still. All the time. I love you, Mom. I miss you. I think you would like this jacket.

I love you,
Kim

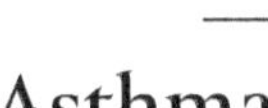

6

—

Asthma

Dear Mom,

I have a cold. As colds go, it feels pretty virulent, swooping in on Thursday evening as a rumble in the chest. I still went to work out, even though I recalled when my grandfather, your father, had a cold and complications related to his lungs and he told me that his father had said to him, "When you don't feel good, work harder." My grandfather was working with that chest cold on the Monday of the week when he went into the hospital on Wednesday and died on Sunday. I went to the gym with this in mind, not because I was interested in working harder (the trainer already works me way harder than I'd like) but because I often put off acknowledging that I might be sick. I was on the cusp. I went to the gym.

I remember in your later years, perhaps when you were over fifty or sixty, you began to get colds fairly often. Maybe from travel, from cold weather, from your history of smoking, or even from some weakness related to your immune system that might be attributable to old trauma and the need to revert to a childlike state. I don't know. I do know the colds came often, and you had a powerful, almost superstitious, fear of getting sick. You would avoid us at all costs if we were ill, or even potentially ill, and then you'd be home, miserable, and sick. I've inherited a bit of that superstition, almost feeling angry if someone is near me with a cold, too frightened of the virus and not confident enough in my own immune system. Today I am sick in that way that just feels bad.

What all of this touches on is that you also died from a weakness in your lungs. Not the cancer that came to get you swiftly and furiously, so fast that our reconciliation couldn't catch up with it. But it was your lungs that ended your life and any hope I still held to be close to you again. You had a cold when you went for chemo after battling through the process of radiation, and when you had your second chemo treatment with a cold, they didn't send you home. Where was your superstition then? Why didn't you stay home with your cold?

The chemo began, your immune system became compromised, they took you to intensive care, they put you on a breathing machine, and they hit you with antibiotics. But whatever the thing was that was attacking your lungs was too strong for you to fight back. And I lost you. Before we could talk.

When I was little, I had asthma. We had late nights together in hospital rooms, scary times when I could not breath at all. I had to learn to surrender, stop fighting to breathe, drop into the fear, and let the lungs begin to open. I learned to tell myself, "Don't panic."

I wish I could stop fighting with your departure, the manner of your death. Not the part about your lungs or the cancer, but the part where you didn't want to see me. I lost you. I loved you. How the hell do I learn to surrender, to stop fighting to breathe through the pain, to drop into the fear, and to let my heart open?

Today, I am sick with a cold, and I am miserable. It's the kind of day when nurturing is called for and nothing will do. It's going to be warm and beautiful outside, and I am going to be here, wrapped in a blanket or sitting in front of a fan, or whatever I have to do to endure, to recover, to get better. Getting over your death is sort of like that. Nothing can be done about it. I'll pull up a blanket, endure, and wait for it to get better.

I love you,
Kim

Kim and Meredith, newly minted Berkeley girls.

7

—

Hare Krishna

Dear Mom,

As this morning's orange sunrise spilled over the Montreal mountains, I was listening to Russell Brand interview Radhanath Swami, and at the end of the podcast, they began to chant. I didn't know what they would chant, and I was surprised and amused when the chant became Hare Krishna, Krishna Krishna, Hare Krishna, Hare Rama, Rama Rama, Hare Rama.

This, for sure, takes me back to our early days in Berkeley. I remember being with you in Sproul Plaza on the Southside of the University of California, Berkeley campus, and the "Hare Krishnas" would be there with their drums, bells, and tambourines, their long orange robes, shaved heads, and dots on their foreheads. They were dancing and chanting that very chant I heard this morning.

As a little girl, it was great fun to jump in and dance and chant along with them. You laughingly encouraged me and supported my participation. The Hare Krishnas were an intrinsic part of the Sproul Plaza/Berkeley landscape at that time, and hearing the chant this morning brought back memories of a joyful exploration

Kim and Meredith as hippie kids.

of all things new and activist in Berkeley. Chanting the Hare Krishna mantra is meant to offer a taste of blissful eternal life beyond birth and death, a potent method of self-realization and spiritual awakening. Certainly, Berkeley offered you a taste of the blissful life beyond the small town where you grew up. You'd made a break, a run for it, and there we were, in 1966, in Berkeley, California. And my sister and I could dance and bounce around and chant and run a little bit wild. I think that made you happy.

I love you, Mom.
Kim

8

—

Boursin

Dear Mom,

Yesterday I had lunch at the home of a man who is a magician and a woman who is a researcher on invasive species. That seems like a combination of interests you would have enjoyed. They served Boursin and Camembert. When I tasted the Boursin, I thought it was probably the most delicious cheese I'd ever had. I didn't know it was a Boursin (I hadn't asked yet) and only knew that it was light, almost fluffy, buttery, creamy, rich, and so tasty. This morning as I reflected on the cheese (isn't morning often a time for reflecting on the previous day's food choices—good and bad?) I found myself, once again, thinking of you. I recall your joy in cheeses.

We were fortunate in North Berkeley that we were there when the Cheese Board opened up, first in the tiny storefront and then later in their bigger location around the corner. 1967 is when they opened that first tiny shop. You reveled in cheese: smelly goat cheese, blue cheese, walnut cheese, cherry cheese, soft cheeses, hard cheeses, cheese fondue, gouda, camembert, brie, gruyere, jack, and that wonderful, made-by-the-Cheese-Board Boursin in quart-size containers. Cheese. And fresh-baked breads and specialty crackers, on beautiful ceramic or hand-blown glass plates—these were all a part of the sense of a European lifestyle that you valued. You loved that we could walk to the shops, the petite shops that grew over time, starting with Peet's Coffee Shop and the small Village Shop gift shop, long before the "gourmet ghetto" existed. This was our home. The inviting Euro-culture of our neighborhood, with its Co-op Grocery Store and later the Charcuterie, the flower stand, and le Poulet. A tiny dream of France on our doorstep.

You gave me the love of those experiences and the daydream of Europe as a place to long for. You made the pleasure of cheese, good bread, food, and flowers all a part of daily life. Small indulgences turned into grand occasions, adventures in small measure, and brought home to share. There was laughter then. Love. Fun. Holidays. The memories of the early days of your marriage to Malcolm, of Aunt Jean newly married and in love with Uncle Phil; we had some semblance of family, and at times, it was good.

This morning I remember last night's good cheese and how it reminded me of a basket of good memories of you and me and Meredith, and memories of Berkeley. We were a unit of sorts, on a journey together, a secret and sublime otherworld away from the bad things, taking in the good things, and able to savor the lightness and richness of life for a time. Thank you for that.

I love you,
Kim

9

—

When You Died

Dear Mom,

I was not in the room when you died. I had come from New Orleans by way of Pennsylvania, thinking I would have three weeks to convince you to see me. I intended to find my way to you. Instead, we lost you.

When I got to the hospital, you were not conscious. Because you had been unwilling to see me while conscious, there was debate and concern about letting me be with you. Thank God Uncle Jerry decided that at that point, my need to be there was worth allowing me to be there—he knew you were unlikely to live much longer. The hospital social worker watched vigilantly; the sense was that I was unstable and might do something bad—it was fucked up. Anyway, I got there with my friend Amy, and you were alone in the room. The social worker first intervened and then hovered. Later, your brother Jerry, your sister Jean, and her husband, Phil, arrived. But still, I had some time alone with you. My own time.

And then in the next day or so, you died. I wasn't there.

I was on my way, and I arrived just after. Jerry asked me if I'd like to see you, and I was given private time. You were still there energetically in the room. I took my hands and moved them along your arms and legs. I helped you clear the energy, and I laid my head on your chest. And I felt you asking me to help my sister. You knew I would.

Even earlier, as you were dying, you feared that Meredith would need help. In fact, when they were carting you by ambulance from the chemo treatment center to the intensive care unit where you would be sedated, you called Meredith to make sure she had your credit card and would be able to stay afloat while you were in the hospital. She did not imagine you wouldn't leave there. You did not seem to imagine that you would not leave there. But you did not leave there.

And in that short time, all was left behind: your home in Davenport on the coast, your friends and extended family in Costa Rica, your Berkeley house and 1960s college memories, your science, your brilliance, your love of art and culture—gone. And me, left by your bedside. Bereft. Unable to summon you. Unable to be with you. Unable to do anything but know your silent, frantic concern: *Please help Meredith.*

And I have. For the twenty years of her marriage to an overbearing and not well person, I listened, I loved, I suspended judgment, and I was there for her. And by some miracle, when you were no longer there to hold the other end of the tug-of-war rope that had you on one end and her husband on the other, it became harder for her to defend him. With you gone and her having direct access to the resources you left her, she had the possibility of independence. Despite her once-firm intention to never leave him, she did. He, thankfully, used drugs. And that turned out to be her "do not cross" line.

Meredith hiking, photographed by a hiking buddy.

Although she had planned to take him back, to resume the foggy dream she had of growing old with him on a porch somewhere, I quietly hoped she would raise the bar higher than just expecting him to stop using. And she carefully, one step at a time, put herself together. I think she cried for two years. Can you imagine? You were gone; her husband was revealed as a thief, liar, and active drug user; her dog died; her children were in distress; she'd spent her adult life torn between you and him—and now you were both gone and she could find herself.

She's amazing. She's kind and loving, determined, strong, and smart. She's super quick with her intelligence, even though she lacks confidence in it. She goes hiking, has a supportive recovery sponsor, enjoys a close circle of women friends, and is raising her children with love and laughter.

I don't know how much you would like her independence, as you most assuredly would have had an opinion about, and tried to control, everything. But I do know you can rest easy, Mom. Meredith is good. She's great. And I love her tremendously. I miss you, and I wish our relationship wasn't left where it was when you died. However, your departure turned out to be perfectly timed for saving Meredith.

I love you,
Kim

Mommy – If you're home by 1 A.M. or 2 A.M. would you please wake me up and give me 2 more aspirin. I'd like to attempt to keep my temperature down so that I can sleep tonight I think today & tomorrow are going to be the worst days of my sickness but perhaps if I keep up the aspirin I'll manage to keep my temprature from being high when I wake up tomorrow and then I can keep it down. If you go to sleep before I am forget it but any time you get home after that please wake me up and give me the aspirin. Please don't wait up to give it to me.
     I hope you got lots and lots of work done.
               Much, much & super much,
               love! Good-night
                    Kim

The note from Kim.

10

Nurture

Dear Mom,

This morning, I had this sense of your presence, at my shoulder, while I still lay in bed. It felt like you were concerned. The energy felt a bit dense. I acknowledged the feeling, maybe out loud, that I felt your concern. And then I began to cry.

I am sick. It's been several days now, and I'm feeling the weight of it. The lonely, alone, and tired-of-being-sick feeling. Also, I am in the middle of a big life change that daunts me. So this feeling of your concern—it touched me. In thinking about this, I recalled a time years ago when Meredith and I were sorting papers for you—you used to pay us to do things like this—and we found a note I had left for you when I was little. It said something like:

Mommy, I hope you had a good night studying at the lab. I am sick. If it's not too much trouble when you get home, will you wake me and take my temperature and give me some baby aspirin?

A different kind of bedtime story. Longing for you then; missing you now. Good night, Mom.

I love you,

Kim

11

—

Rupture

Dear Mom,

You, me, Meredith—we had a tight bond. But somewhere in there, you began to separate us. You divided us into two twosomes instead of one threesome.

In 2005, when I was returning from my fellowship at the Kennedy Center, Meredith and I had a phone call. She was going to spend the weekend with you in Davenport, perhaps even to help you sort belongings, and she was scared to go. She was afraid she would over-confide in you about the difficulty of being married to her husband. I suggested that I join you both. I told her that you and I were in a really good place. I had called you often while I was in Washington, DC, and we'd been enjoying a close long-distance relationship. She and I thought that was an excellent solution. We'd have fun, she'd keep some boundaries, and I would get to see you too. All good.

Except it wasn't. You asked Meredith to ask me not to come. And I was not willing to accept that.

A very interesting thing happened while I was at the Kennedy Center. I had found a new value for myself. My new self did not think it was okay to be uninvited to a family gathering. That is not what polite people do. That is not how I wanted to be treated. That is not what a mother does. A mother says, "I am happy to see you," even if she had hoped to have time alone with her other daughter.

In response to you, I said that I was taking a big step back to process this un-invitation. I don't think I knew how to react. I felt furious. I felt hurt. I felt unprepared for this rejection. I told you I would be shutting down communication in order to consider how I felt and what to do. You moved into gear. This was not the outcome you wanted. You called, changing the playing field and breaking the boundary I had just set when I asked for time to consider my feelings.

You asked me to come on the Saturday or Sunday after Meredith was gone. You said you wanted to see me. You said it wasn't fair, that I was punishing you, and that you were going to Costa Rica and I should see you before you left. You just wanted to see us one on one, and I should understand that. You moved the goal posts and won. I agreed to come see you. And then another development occurred. The night before I was supposed to come there, I felt dread. I felt fear. And I paid attention to those feelings. I told myself I did not have to go and see anyone I was afraid of—my mother or anyone else.

And so I called and told you I wasn't coming. I explained that I was taking a step back. That I loved you but something inside of me had to take care of me. You were not happy with my choice.

Having made that decision, I felt a shift in my emotional life. My teenage self made an appearance. The child who had run away for extended periods, always being dragged back by the ear, spoke up and said, "Finally. Finally I can keep my promise to myself to never go back." All those years of being beaten and shamed by you, and being impotent to change things, now became an opportunity to protect myself in my adult life. Still, the fear remained. I promised myself that I did not have to go back. I could allow myself to not see you until I worked through the fear.

It isn't that I did not want to process these experiences with you. In fact, over the years, I tried many times. I finally realized that you could not process the past with me, and I finally took personal responsibility for the repair work I needed to do for myself. I felt, clearly, that I could not have the refrain of your point of view about me surrounding me while I sorted myself out. I needed to dismantle and rebuild on my own.

I understand that my decision felt like abandonment to you. I understand that this felt to you like I took the financial support you gave me to do the fellowship and never looked back, ungrateful and seemingly unrepentant, and that I hurt you. That wasn't my intention. I wanted to heal. I wanted to be strong enough to love you. Because I always, always loved you. I was just scared shitless.

In the years that followed, I faltered and grew stronger. It was super hard at first. I tried to reach out to you about a year or two later, but you did not respond. My sister would tell me about encounters with you, and it still sounded unhealthy, so I felt some need to stay distant. After more years went by, I knew I was ready to reconnect. I knew I was strong enough. I had never stopped missing you or loving you.

I tried to reach out, tentatively, with a birthday card in January 2013. You didn't respond. Meredith encouraged me to call you, but I was too scared. In 2014, the desire to reach out to you became more pressing. I tried harder. I sent a card, a gift, and an email, and finally, I got an email back from you. We had an exchange of emails: me, you, then me, then you, then me, then you, then me, then silence. After that, I only had news of your illness, your refusal to have contact with me, and then your death.

I saved and printed those emails. Little tiny signs of life and love between us. They were the proof to show that you might be open to my being at your deathbed, to my being with you while you transitioned.

Now, I cannot change any of it. But I can sometimes feel your presence and concern, as I did recently when I woke up feeling sick and felt your presence by my shoulder.

> I love you, Mom.
> I miss you.
> Kim

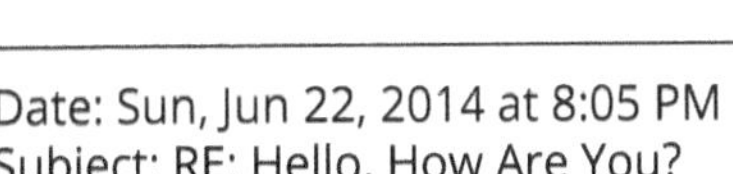

Date: Sun, Jun 22, 2014 at 8:05 PM
Subject: RE: Hello, How Are You?
To: Kim Cook

Hi Kim, thank you for the nice card, book and email. I enjoy hearing about your life in NO.

When I heard you were going there I thought it would be perfect knowing your personal and professional interests, as well as your creative heart and ability to help NO rebuild it's life.

A perfect match, I think. Change is always difficult, and so it was for me moving from BRK to Pasadena.

But what a good decision it was for me. Similarly, I think and hope NO will end up making you very happy! I don't know what a shotgun house is, but will look on Google.

Sorry I tire rather easily and I have so much to do. I will write more later. But meanwhile I am optimistic because I have the best doctors at UCSF.

Thanks again for your warm and generous letter,

Love,
Mom

An email correspondence between Kim and her mom from 2014.

12

——

Afterlife

Dear Mom,

Is there an afterlife? I know what you would have said, what you did say, when you were alive. You, with your firm commitment to science, would say, "No evidence. Body decomposes." I thought you would have been cremated. Instead, you opted for a traditional burial in your hometown graveyard near your parents.

Now that you are dead, I think there is an afterlife and I think you're experiencing it. It feels to me like you are now the essence of wildflowers and butterflies, your genetic afterlife code. The energy therein is now your presence. Wildflowers and butterflies.

Remember when we lived in Clovis, on Clovis Avenue, with the irrigation ditch on one side and the big open field past our yard in the back? Remember how much you loved wildflowers, and I would go and pick them for you when I was like three or five? This is still you. Wildflowers and butterflies. You cultivated a wild abandon of a garden at your home by the Pacific Ocean in the little town of Davenport, where they lit a candle for you and placed it at the staff workstation in the Whaler restaurant, where

Kim with wildflowers.

I saw it from the counter when I went in the week after you died.

I feel you. You enter into my energy field, you come into my dreams, you try to impress things upon me. You might be haunting me. I am not sure. You might be wanting something different at the finish of our story. I know I do. I used to dream of our house on fire and overflowing toilets; there was so much fury and chaos and confusion and fear in our house then. Now, my dreams of you are mostly about connecting, grief, and losing you. Again.

In my dreams, you are evoked and living inside the blending of our two lives. You are everywhere in who I am. This is remarkable, visceral. I know I am not you, but we are still somehow connected in your afterlife. Energetically, it feels like the enmeshed weird boundary-breaking nature of our emotional entanglement is waning. As it fades, I'm trying to strike a balance between good ways you imprinted on me and the not-so-healthy learned coping mechanisms that need updating. I think you are alive somehow. Not really able to communicate, perhaps a bit surprised and delighted to discover this new realm to explore, and definitely refuting the intellectual scientific basis for your belief that there was no life after death. You seem willing to shed that as less consequential in favor of the bigger picture. It turns out you are discovering there is more science. More physics out there in this new dimension. More remarkable knowledge to learn.

Wow, what a mind you had. I miss the ability to connect with you in your actual life. There may be an afterlife. I feel an essence and presence of you. Wildflowers and butterflies. Your presence comes to me carrying tendrils of hope that we are finding a form of peace even though you are gone. I wonder whether that feeling is my imagined landscape, more interior than real. Whichever it is, you are there and here, and I feel you.

I love you, Mom.
Kim

13

Books

Dear Mom,

One of the greatest gifts you gave me was a joy in books. My earliest memories involve books. Trips in the vivid heat to the small-town Clovis Carnegie Library, a tiny stucco yellow building that opened in 1915 with high ceilings and hardwood floors. We would climb the steps to the front door, and sometime later, I would emerge with a stack of books. This going to the library and emerging with a giant stack of books continued when we got to Berkeley. That library was much bigger, grand, and beautiful. It had high ceilings and large glass windows illuminated by sunlight cast down on the large reading room with wooden tables on wooden floors. It was built in 1934, not that I knew that then. I was only conscious of the rows and rows of bookshelves, at my height, filled with books. I read every folk tale, fairy tale, and myth in the library; I discovered a grand passion for Greek mythology and pursued that road as far as it would take me.

The library was one entry point to books, but you provided others. You gave me a book allowance. You went to the little bookstore that adjoined the Berkeley Co-op Grocery Store on Shattuck Avenue and put $15 a month on deposit for me and another $15 for Meredith. That must have been a fortune for you on your college student budget. It was a marvelous gift for me—and probably helped you when you were grocery shopping because Meredith and I could spend our time deciding how to spend our book allowance.

By the time I was nine, I had a college-level reading ability. I am not sure how I know this, but I do know that my intelligence was a clearly stated part of my childhood. You focused on speaking about and making it evident that I was smart. I am not sure for what purpose, and I came to resent the feeling that it was all you saw of me, but by now, I understand the huge gift that turned out to be. Impressing upon a young girl that she is unquestionably smart has lasting benefits. Given that I could read at an advanced level, you gave me access to all of your books. You had more than one wall filled with shelves and filled with books. Here are some of the titles I remember for sure that I read between about ages nine and twelve:

- The Collected Works of Shakespeare
- *Mein Kampf* by Adolf Hitler
- *Che* (not sure now who authored that one)
- *Justine* and *Juliette* by the Marquis de Sade
- *Lady Chatterley's Lover* by D.H. Lawrence
- *Siddhartha*, and I think *Steppenwolf*, by Hermann Hesse
- *Soledad Brother: The Prison Letters of George Jackson*
- *Seize the Time* by Bobby Seale
- *Soul on Ice* by Eldridge Cleaver

There were others, but these are a few of the ones that remain in memory. It's pretty funny that I was able to access those titles before I became a teenager. I also remember that someone gave me *The Chronicles of Narnia* books in those years, and by the time my adolescence was completed, I'd read them fourteen times.

In many ways, this reading ties into my asthma, my confusion at the chaotic world unfolding around us, and my extremely shy nature. So, it was books. Always books. My father, when I would visit him, was annoyed by this lost-in-books quality, with me on the couch, lost in a book, while others watched football games in winter and had fun swimming outside in summer. Out of books came my advanced vocabulary, and my stepsisters said I used too many big words. They didn't want me to play with them or their friends.

For you, there was no such thing as too many big words—the more the merrier when it came to my vocabulary. My precocity was your delight. And well into my adulthood, a shared activity with you was a trip to the bookstore, where you could be counted on to spend hundreds of dollars on the stack of books I was inevitably drawn to. You turned me on to books you liked, from Oliver Sacks to Sue Grafton—not that I read them all. In the years before you died, when we were not in contact, I discovered Canadian mystery writer Louise Penny. I kept the series, planning to share them with you. I was never able to do that. I think you would have loved them. When Uncle Jerry held your memorial, he had all the books from your home staged in shelves in the light industrial warehouse space adjoining his offices. All those in attendance were invited to take the books they wanted—this was at your direction from your will—and afterward, the rest were to be donated to the Clovis Library. The books were going back to where we started, the Clovis Library.

I perused the books, looking for the *Whole Earth Catalog,* which I know you had, but could not find it. In any case, I did see the Adelle Davis book *Let's Eat Right to Keep Fit,* with memories of our morning "Pep-Up" in our early days in Berkeley. I didn't find anything substantially interesting or meaningful, just lots of books. Then your friend, Dick, found *A Pattern Language* by Christopher Alexander. That was amazing! I'd been told many times that I should read that book—having begun a deep exploration of public space and how we construct the built environment. He wanted it but saw my response, and he gave it to me. I was thankful to receive it. Almost, but not quite, feeling like it was a topic of interest we shared with each other, or would have shared. You and I would have discussed its contents. It became one more book shared between us.

This idea, like many others, is hard to let go of: this sharing of books with you. You and Dick also had this sharing. He came to visit me in New Orleans the year after you died. Well, to be clear, he came for a conference and asked to see me. We met for dinner, and he spoke to me of his regret. He regretted not having been more adamant with you about seeing me. He regretted it more because now he knew me, and he told me how much he saw you in me. I am cerebral, kind, and caring in a way that you failed to see, and I, for sure, reflect many qualities that are directly linked to you. And to books. Our shared love of books. To knowledge, learning, and the big wide world. Wow, you gave me all that. Thank you.

> I love you, Mom.
> Kim

Mavis McClure sculpture in Kim's garden.

14

—

Stuff

Dear Mom,

I was just unloading the dishwasher and saw a kitchen utensil, shiny bright and not that useful, that came from your house. I thought about stuff, about my own need to go through some stuff and let go of stuff, and about all the stuff you had. I lightly laughed in memory.

Remember the time when I came to your home in Clovis? You had gone back and purchased a second home there, a place your brother built, and it sat on ten acres or more. You had a vision to create a kind of artist residency there. You took horseback riding lessons and imagined putting horses on the adjacent lot. Big ideas for the future combined with a bit of fantasy regression into your past. I came to visit you, and your place was packed with stuff. It was incredible. I couldn't quite breathe because it felt like it was so compressed.

There was a larger-than-life Mavis McClure sculpture of a male figure from the torso up. There were hand-painted chairs from South America with straw-woven seats buried under large stacks of *The New York Times*. There were antique credenzas and dressers. The baby grand player piano from your mother that you fully restored. Furniture, artworks, musical instruments, art deco lamps, books, old newspapers, and cats climbing over all of it. Belongings distributed around the room in a hectic mélange of hopes and dreams not fulfilled but promised. Memories and fantasies mingled together in one huge explosion of your psychic content. You had even more possessions in storage than I saw in your home. So. Much. Stuff. You were collecting dreams for your future and preserving your past, leaving no room for anything to actually take place there.

We went to lunch at the slightly self-conscious (okay, a lot self-conscious) Old Town Cafe (of sorts – nothing like the cafés of North Berkeley in spite of the name) and discussed life. You told me you were reading a book called *Your Brain on Love*, which was all about the science of love. You shared that you wanted love in your life, meaning romantic love. I gently mentioned the stuff. All the stuff. And that it felt to me like all the stuff, all that used to be and could be, was taking up so much space, literally and energetically, that it might be in the way of finding any space for love. I urged you to let go.

And a bit later, you did. You began to unburden yourself. You heard me, and you began releasing. A mighty river of things began flowing downhill. And you wanted me to catch them. Meredith aided you in going through your storage, your belongings. You even sold that extra house in Clovis, and you kept asking me to take some of the stuff. It was beautiful. It was valuable. It was a gift from you to me. I said, "No thank you." Consistently. Clearly. This made you mad. You sent me some stuff anyway. Three art deco lamps you thought I would like. And, of course, now I have your shiny kitchen utensils.

It was incomprehensible to you that I was stepping aside and letting the flow roll past me.

This was about fifteen years before you died. Even after releasing your river of things, you managed to buy even more before you died. More beautiful stuff. Joyful expressions of moments of love and treasures that you sought and found. It turns out that you did not find romantic love.

When your wishes were read out loud after your death—there was no stuff for me. All your personal property was left to my sister. Ouch. I had actually loved and appreciated your stuff. Yet I had no rights to it— not only to the belongings but more importantly, to the process. People were able to come in, clean up, and push my sister to hurry up and sell everything at an estate sale, where they cast doubt on the value of your stuff.

The Mavis McClure from Clovis was gone, but there were other items worth tens of thousands of dollars. No one saw value in the stuff. It was too much work to manage the stuff and determine its value; time to move it along. Meredith wanted to slow down, but she was overwhelmed. I wanted her to be able to take time to assess the value and get the most money she could—she would need all she could get for her family. Art resellers were contacted; they do know the value but retain most of it for themselves. Eventually, it was too much to handle, so Meredith let much of it go in various ways.

I did get some of your stuff. I don't know if you didn't want me to have any; you certainly didn't leave it to me. I wanted to cherish your stuff that had been lovingly collected. I didn't want to keep it as much as I wanted to make the distributing of it more sacred and less disposal.

Meredith was kind to me: I have a rug, some artwork, a small Mavis McClure, some dishes I love, a table, a side table, some kitchenware (like shiny utensils), and your LPs. I got some stuff. I hope you would want me to have it. I wish you had left me the rights to share in your possessions along with Meredith. Did you think she was the only one who cared? Did you think she was the one who needed it most? Did you think that because I didn't want your items fifteen years earlier, I wouldn't want to keep some of them or assist with the process after you were gone? I don't know. I'm not sure it matters.

Sometimes, it feels like the manner of your death and your wishes upon your death have de-legitimized my daughter-ness. That I can't claim to be your daughter in the same way my sister can. Somehow, my memories, my love for you, my life with you, and my claim to you do not seem valid. That hurts. I think about it while I load the dishwasher.

> I love you, Mom. I wish
> we could talk about this.
> Kim

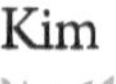

15

———

Santería

Dear Mom,

Remember when I was nineteen and I was initiated into Santería? That was the night you shared the memory of your first sexual experience, well actually, trauma, with me. You lived in Southern California, in a sort of house in the woods in Tujunga, and I was coming to Los Angeles to be initiated by my Cuban Madrina and Padrino, Marcus and Mimi. You were relatively sanguine about my choice to join this African traditional religion, unlike my sister, who was, at the time, a born-again Christian and told me she was not going to be able to speak to me again as I was a pagan and going to hell. Fortunately, she changed her mind about all that later. In your case, maybe you just found my choice more interesting, plus you had a very strong antipathy toward fundamentalist Christians. In any case, you made me feel welcome to stay in your home after my ceremony.

I arrived, dressed in white with my head wrapped, after a full day of secret ritual followed by a bembé of drumming, chanting, and dancing. I was vibrating at some super high level, full of energy, goodness, and a feeling of love running through my body. You were at

Mom in a high school photo.

home, quietly, with your brother Jerry and sister-in-law Suzanne. I think, somehow, my experience brought an openness into the room. And as we sat and talked, the conversation unfolded into this story.

This story of how you had a boyfriend in high school. And you broke up with him. Yet, he pursued you. And then, one night, when you had been bowling with your friends and left the building afterward, your car wouldn't start. This boy—this not-a-friend—offered to help you out and give you a ride home. You thought this was a safe choice. It was not. He took you far out into the farmland, down a dark and distant road, and he pulled a knife on you. His plan was to kill you, based on the reasoning that you didn't love him, and if he couldn't have you, then no one could. You begged. You pleaded. You lied. You persuaded. You told him you loved him. And you proved it by giving him your virginity. And even forty years later, as you told this story, you felt you had defiled yourself. Cheapened yourself. Whored yourself. But you saved your life. You made it home.

And then, you married my father. Who, you told us as you continued to confide in us, had persistently asked you if you were a virgin before he married you. And after many nights of his drunken conviction that you only belonged to him if you had been a virgin when you married, you gave up. You confessed that you were not a virgin. After that, he continued to torment you, punishing you with accusations and drunkenness. You started sleeping on the couch and denying him sex. He molested me. He fondled me. He scared me. Eventually, he pulled a gun on you, and you left him.

Years later, when I entered puberty, you began to call me a whore. You called me disgusting and inappropriate. How was I to know what you were carrying? How you had blamed yourself? Or how so much of that was translating into your rejection of me? Mom, you saved your life. You lived. You even managed to leave my father and carry your two daughters to safety beyond that small town. Although I can't quite say you survived it.

I love you, Mom.
Kim

16

—

Me Too

Dear Mom,

I'm watching *CBS News Sunday Morning* this morning, and they did an interview with Mariska Hargitay, who plays a character on *Law and Order: Special Victims Unit* about sex crimes. They discuss how playing this role has spilled over into her real life as an advocate for victims and women's issues. They refer to her as the "godmother" of the Me Too movement.

Sexual assault is a complicated issue for you and me. Around 2002, I was spending about ten days with you on the coast in Davenport. We felt close. So I read you some poems I wrote, including one about Dad. It's a pretty crushing poem. Here's a bit of it:

My first romance was a difficult one
My father
I still think of him with a hazy glow, a sense of desire for his smile, his attention.
I feel a sort of wistful attraction to his aw shucks, easy grace and humor.
A fairy tale that is partly true.
How I miss him, how I long for his love.

Daddy

*I remember your rude fingers reaching out to pinch
the budding breasts of each of my sisters and me in
turn as we flowered.*

Daddy

Other parts of the poem were even more crushing.

The next morning, I was on the lower deck of your house, and you came out to the upper deck, and you started to express your distress. You had a few concerns; you were worried that I would go to local recovery meetings and talk about my life. The Daddy poem wasn't the only one I had shared with you; I also shared some writing about my relationship with you. I had thought we were at an open, trusting moment. Apparently, you felt so attacked that the next morning, you said you had spent the night wanting to kill yourself because of my poems. This urge to kill yourself was not new. Now I understand more about how this threat of suicide, the intense internal collapse into extreme pain, was a part of your experience. It came from your own trauma. That day, what I felt was my own extreme feeling of rejection. You went on to say that you were certain what I wrote about my father was not true. That I had condemned him without the benefit of a fair hearing.

I was furious, I was frightened, I was devastated. I couldn't leave fast enough. I drove up Highway 1 so fast that I got a ticket. I didn't care. I had to put distance between me and you and your determined denial of my experience. And here's the thing. We didn't even get into your boyfriend George and what happened to me when I was eight and we went with him to Santiago, Chile. So here goes.

Back then, you had a lover named Pierre. You were beautiful. He was handsome and fun. He drove a TR6, and we would go for McDonald's french fries with the top down. Two little girls in the back, and you and he in the front. (Side note: I recently found Jacques Brel albums with Pierre's name on them among your LPs.) And then, enter George. George was dating your friend Michelle, who, by the way, had introduced you to Pierre. You and Pierre were together, and Michelle and George were together. Turns out George wanted you, and Michelle wanted Pierre. Pierre decided that returning to France and the life he was intended for took precedence over whatever love it was that you and he shared. So, Pierre broke up with you. You collapsed emotionally and were hospitalized. The terminology at the time was "nervous breakdown." I think it was this same collapse, this internal default into extreme pain and self-abandonment, that recurred again and again for you. George came to your side at the hospital, whispering his love. You left the hospital, and we packed up and went with George to Chile.

George was a sadist. In your bedroom, the only separation between the two of you and my sister and me was a louvered door. No sound protection. We heard you, and him, and your tears at night.

One day, you and he went to the university, and I had a plan to go and visit a friend. I asked if I could visit my friend, and you said yes. You may have meant, vaguely, "Sometime, yes." But to me, it was much more specific. I set out across the long yard to the big front gate and

Mom at the beach in Chile.

headed to the dusty road. Suddenly, Margarita, who took care of us and the house, grabbed me by the ear. Yelling at me in Spanish, she would not let me go. Of course, she knew that a little eight-year-old blond girl walking down a dusty road outside Santiago in early 1970s Chile would not be safe. But I just knew she was getting in the way of my determination to go visit my friend, and I felt full of the authority vested in me by your approval of this plan. I flailed, I insisted, and then I slapped Margarita. My denial and insistence that I was treated unjustly still make it unclear to me whether I took a stand and coldly slapped her or whether, in my efforts to break free of her firm grip on my ear, I simply swung wildly enough to hit her. I'd like to think the latter, but usually, the portrait of me as a little girl was defined more along the lines of the former. A mean, difficult, troubled child.

That night. When you got home. I was in trouble. I had been confined to my room, waiting for my punishment. I could hear voices when you and George arrived home, so I knew that decisions were being made about my consequences. What I could not have imagined is that George would be given permission to punish me. With all you knew about him, how could that have happened?

George entered that room, standing in the doorway between where he slept with, and beat, you, and the room where I slept and heard those things. I was defiant at first, and I told him he was not my mother and did not have any rights with regard to me. He told me he had your permission.

I think that moment broke me.

Somewhere.

Inside.

For a very long time.

Maybe still.

You turned your back on me. You betrayed me (and I note as I write this that you often used the language of betrayal aimed at me). How?

He took off his belt. He gave me a set of rules. If I took off my clothes, lay on the bed, and did not cry, he would hit me five times. If I took off my clothes, lay on the bed, and cried, he would hit me ten times. If I did not take off my clothes and I cried, he would hit me fifteen times.

I tried. I tried to take off my clothes and not cry. I could not. I cried. I peed on myself. He hit me a lot of times. Memory doesn't tell me what else he did to me.

Margarita, chastened and saddened, I think, by what happened, brought me food on a tray. I threw the whole thing out the window. I was full of pain. I was full of rage. I stayed that way for a very long time.

Four years later when I was twelve, a doctor examined me after I started my period, discovered I had hemorrhoids, and asked about sexual assault. The doctor suggested I was quite young to have them. In any case, it is unknown whether he raped me. I suspect that he did. Regardless, I was deeply, deeply wounded by that experience.

So. Back to 2002, when you wanted to kill yourself because of my poetry. Because of my honesty. I couldn't take it. I drove off.

And I know that you suffered sexual trauma of your own. You knew intellectually what suffering and trauma and sexual assault and discrimination were all about. Yet you could not accept that any of those things had happened to me.

This is super hard stuff. Some of the hardest in our history. It's not the worst, but it's not good, either. To talk about this would have been helpful.

> I love you, Mom. I am
> so sorry for your pain.
> Kim

Kim at Christmas, 13 or 14 years old.

17

—

Seismic

Dear Mom,

I'm wanting to lie down and cry every day right now. I've made big shifts in my life recently, and it's breaking me up. I am thinking of you and your work in seismology because the word "seismic" comes to mind. Seismic shifts. Your research in plate tectonics and earthquake science had a literal meaning for us—we understood a lot more about earthquakes since we lived in shaky, quaky California.

Your work had a profound impact on us, in that it took all you had and more to achieve what you did, and "all you had and more" includes what it took from my sister and me. For a metaphorical meaning, the ground was not stable underneath us. Ever. While that has clearly contributed to my resilience, it is also a part of how difficult it is for me to experience change. It is so destabilizing that I can barely come through it.

One would think that I would just find a place to hunker down and hold tight. Duck and cover. Instead, my drive to grow overwhelms my need to shelter, and I struggle through on hands and knees to pull myself across each chasm of my wounded, petrified, unable-to-function self that cracks open as I reach for the other side.

Liquefaction. The earth's crust is not so firm. I understand the language of geophysics. I live it. Thank you, Mom. I know you sacrificed.

I love you,
Kim

18

—

The Beach

Dear Mom,

There was the ocean. The Pacific Ocean. What a gift to us. As very little girls, my sister and I would go with you to Huntington Beach and visit your uncle, who rode his scooter out on the pier, telling stories of old. When we were a little older, we added beach memories of Half Moon Bay, picnics and sunbathing, and your friend Michelle, always so elegant. And her son Jerome, me, Meredith, and other little friends were running and tumbling, screaming and playing with waves.

Then I added beach memories from your marriage to Malcolm going to Mendocino. That was a true oasis of a place that we visited many times. In my high school years, we went to the Santa Cruz Beach Boardwalk with you and the neighbor Toni, and I remember the roller coaster rides, blankets, setting up home base on the beach, and long days in the sun.

The beach signals a safe space to me. The drive between Half Moon Bay and Davenport, where you eventually made your home for the last thirty years or so of your life, symbolically became what felt like home to me. Driving that road to your house when I got married there with a

*Malcolm, Mom, and Meredith at the beach
in Mendocino, California.*

view of the cliffs and the ocean, to the strawberry fields where I went to pick strawberries—even when I was not welcome to visit you, I could go there.

The ocean—abiding, beautiful, air that replenishes, light that fills my eyes, sounds of soothing waves, and endless, vast blue beauty. You fought with the coastal commission, working to protect the ocean shores. You laid seismographs on the ocean floor in Monterey Bay, thinking about the earth's continental plates and how they moved. You brought us to Berkeley where, at night from the top bunk bed, I could look out across the bay and see the Golden Gate. I've tried living in other places, and always this ocean, this shore, this harbor is where I find home. I am as attached as a starfish in a tidal pond, holding on tightly, to you, to me, to my history here, to the place I call home.

I love you,
Kim

Grandma with Meredith and Kim.

19

Always Love

Dear Mom,

One time I was at the chiropractor's office. She was a network chiropractor, so I lay there for a long time and a lot of energy got moved. In this session, as I lay there, I felt like I was visited by your mother. She was asking me to have mercy on you. She was emanating her love and concern for you in a vibration of red roses and white gardenias and purple hydrangeas, her own garden in wave form.

Your mother was love. She was love and concert pianist and educator to the developmentally differently abled. She was submission. She was fear. She was victim to the blows your father dealt. I don't think anyone came out of that home without deep damage. Wounds deep enough to move through generations. Your mother gave me solace, and hair washed over the sink, and bangs cut with a straight edge of scotch tape and scissors, and nighttime baths with one foot over the edge of the tub at a time to limit the water droplets on the floor, and toilet paper put carefully over the seat when no toilet seat covers were available in public places like the Roeding Park Zoo, and Easter dresses for Easter Sunday church and Easter baskets. And surprise gifts in the bags kept in her closet, and reaching in to pull out a book of connect the dots or a game of jacks, and sitting beside her on the piano bench as she played classical music, Bach, Brahms, Beethoven, and soundtrack scores from *The Sound of Music*, and a Formica red kitchen table with matching picnic-style tablecloths. And always, be careful, don't make him mad. And always love.

I love you, Mom.
Lots of this hurts.
Kim

20

Seeking You

Dear Mom,

After you died, I wanted to retrieve you. I tried. Like, maybe, a research project. I contacted your therapist to see if she could help me understand. She had written a letter to the court to help free your assets from the IRS because you hadn't filed for many years before you died, and I got access to the information in that letter. It was your brother's effort to establish your limitations legally so that your estate didn't go up in smoke (or in this case, taxes). I thought maybe she could tell me more.

She consulted her mentors and legal advisors, and it turns out your confidentiality survived you. I felt impotent. I wanted to protest. To insist. I needed to understand. More and better. But I left it alone due to boundaries and respect. I spent a little time with your friend Dick. It was lovely. He misses you. We couldn't really be friends. I wanted to meet his wife. His dog. It seems his wife was not comfortable with that.

As part of my search for you, I listened acutely to what your sister had to say, but when she said she didn't feel grief but relief at your death, then she did not seem like such a good source. Her expressions of sympathy and support for me weren't substantial enough to overcome her antipathy for you, and my loyalty to you made it difficult to hear her feelings. Although, to be fair, she had a long history of feeling overshadowed by you and had her own wounds to contend with. Your brother's partner also shared with me details about your rage, your anger, your neediness, and your controlling nature. And how you shared with others about me. To sum it up, based on things you said, I was supposed to be a bitch, and it turned out to be a revelation to her that I was not.

I thought about your old friends, and I visited Gail but found her deep in drink and a limited source of information. I looked for contact information for Michelle without luck. Toni feels so loyal to you that she won't speak to me—I'm aggravated by her sense of whatever for you, which adds up her total wall with me. And then our old family friend, David, lovely, well meaning, and caring, but not a useful resource either. I thought about your former long-term lover, who left you and left you feeling desperately at the edge of self-destruction. I could talk to him, but it feels like that would make you furious and hurt.

Where can I find you—in some letters, some photos, some belongings? In my memories? It's a lot, this losing of you.

I love you, Mom.
Kim

21

—

Laszlo Products

Dear Mom,

This morning as I washed my face, I was reminded of the time when you discovered Erno Laszlo products. You bought hundreds of dollars of specialty Laszlo and sent it to me and Meredith. It was a funny way that you tried to do retroactive parenting as we became older. It was sweet, really. Bursts of enthusiasm at something you were certain would be helpful. In this case, facial care. And when you discovered the book *Rich Dad Poor Dad* and were positive that my sister and I could gain something from it, you had a big swing in favor of the value of budgeting.

At one point, you asked me to assign you a grade as a parent. Presumably as an intellectual and a professor, you thought this was a reasonable way to evaluate parenting. I gave you an A for intellectual stimulation but stuttered through trying to state the not-passing grade for emotional empathy and nurturing. Still, as I reflect on your parenting, I know that you were interested in being a mother, even well past my childhood. It's not possible to take an "incomplete" and then make up the course later. But it is possible to convey that you care. And you did. Thank you, Mom.

I love you,
Kim

22

—

Weight

Dear Mom,

Wow. I remember when you were young. I remember when you began to age. I remember how I felt about you: embarrassed, distressed, confused. I remember when you went from sexy, desirable, and beautiful to square, solid, sexless, and heavy. I was ashamed when I saw you devouring a chocolate-covered strawberry at a dance concert when I was on tour with a hip-hop dance company. Somehow, I saw your evident pleasure in the food as a bad reflection on me as you stood there, no longer light and attractive. I am sad now at the cruelty of that judgment.

I remember feeling distanced from you when you came to my theater in San Francisco with your friend. Your delight and pleasure in the success of the evening was evident, but I was stiff and not welcoming. *What the fuck. What the motherfuck, more like. Fucking shit.* What was I thinking? Some twisted backward sense of value based on appearance got all mixed up with my antipathy and merged identity, blended in with some out-of-date puberty reaction at being seen with my mom, and fully loaded with gender norms and social codes that you tried to rise above.

I remember you talking about the disadvantages of being attractive or desirable as a woman in science, saying that men would not take you seriously if you were beautiful. As you aged, your jaw jutted out further, your stance got more determined, your body rounded out. I had the wrong lens on all that. I, wounded and self-centered and emotionally underdeveloped, put up an arm's length distance of disdain and judgment. That was fucked up. I am sure you felt it. I deeply regret those moments, those choices. Because in those moments, you were showing up, and I fell short. I'm sorry.

I love you, Mom. Really.

Kim

23

Gender

Dear Mom,

Recently I created a backstory for a creative project that included a character who is a gender-fluid poet physicist. It is causing me to reflect on the conversations you and I had over the years with regard to gender, starting with you giving me the names Robin and Kim and wanting my names to be gender-nonspecific. You didn't tell me why you wanted my names to be detached from being female; you only told me that it was an intentional choice.

You and gender. Your frequent topic of discussion was how you were limited in your field because of your sex. You were very clear that to be seen as sexual was a disadvantage in science. Over time, you discovered a gender-neutral outfit, one fitting for a field scientist who also worked in the lab, and you wore it consistently. Gradually, your femininity faded away in terms of how you presented yourself.

You often talked about the disadvantages of being passed over for better positions because you were both a woman and older due to your first marriage and your children delaying your entry into the university. If your father had allowed you to go to Stanford after you were accepted there, how different life would have been. You were born in 1940, and much of the freedoms you provided for me, perhaps most significantly the liberty of believing in my own intelligence, were not offered to you.

When you did your postdoc at CalTech, there were no women professors in the sciences, and after five years, they did not offer you a professor's position and the clock had run out on the postdoc options. You sat in your chair and cried. Tears streamed down your face. You couldn't function. You had to spend time in the hospital. A mental incapacity to accept this rejection.

You were deeply afraid and consequently wounded at the idea of the department secretary as a desirable archetype, who, to your mind, was without brains and dressed to attract men. When your lover of fourteen years left you for the department secretary, you, again, lost your senses in despair for a long time. This lover you had met at CalTech got offers at Harvard and U.C. Berkeley while you got offers at Stonybrook College and U.C. Santa Cruz. You saw this as a matter of gender. Never mind that ultimately, you would win the National Medal of Honor for your work in Costa Rica.

This topic of gender, feminism, femininity, and opportunity is a heavy one. You had much to say about it in a bitter sort of way—castigating men who dated women who were, in your estimation, less intelligent. You felt that men want to fuck women who are less intelligent. For you, if they want to fuck you, they will not respect your science.

You were fierce. You were determined. You fought for every inch of your progress. I know that we struggled, you and I. You were not comfortable with my pronounced femininity. Holy shit, I was all pink, and makeup, and I-wanna-take-ballet. You certainly sneered at me with my ways, standing in the bathroom door and making fun of me while I put on makeup. Perhaps you were actually in fear for me. I know the price I paid in your battle for your own life. I see how very hard it was to accomplish what you did. I do know that you carried me and my sister with you out of the small-town world that closed you in and transported us all into the world of books, ideas, art, world culture, political activism, and yes, feminism. Thank you.

> I love you, Mom.
> You are amazing. I wish
> we could talk about
> these things now.
> Kim

Kim, Mom, and Meredith "in drag" for visits to family.

24

Keeping Secrets

Dear Mom,

Well. One thing was very clear: Do not tell.

> Do not tell *your* father about
> Your lovers
> The drugs
> Or anything at all
>
> Do not tell *my* father about
> Your lovers
> The drugs
> Or anything at all

When put on the spot, which happened regularly, lie. Visiting Dad and Grandpa included protracted Q and A sessions about our lives. It garnered me a reputation in the family as a liar—not that it was the only bad quality attributed to me. Still, this one was considered a given. Kim is a liar.

Then there was the part of my life that started to get really bad. Molestation bad. Stringy hair and dirty neck bad. Teased at school bad. Shoplifting bad. Stuff like that. After we had lived in South America and returned home,

I told my stepsister, who told her mother, who told my father, about what happened to me with your boyfriend. Well, Dad took me into his bedroom, and in a horrible reenactment, he took off his belt and threatened me with it if I didn't tell him whether what I told my stepsister was true. I told him it was true.

Then he confronted you, and we had to go and live with him for six months. You considered me as having betrayed you. Why did I make up all those lies? That's what you wanted to know. I wrote you a letter of apology, saying that I know you were like the little engine that could, and I was on the back, in the caboose, dragging my feet and slowing you down. I cried for so long that year. I was in fourth grade. I would stand in line to go into the classroom, but they'd have to take me to the administrative office because I couldn't stop crying. The teacher finally reached me with spelling bees. I liked those.

Later, when I was older, I tried telling the women who were our next-door neighbors about how you were treating me. They, concerned, asked you about it. You would cry and ask me why I made up such stories about you.

Around my fifth grade year, you started me in therapy at Children's Hospital. The doctor's name was Marjory something. I spent a long time refusing to talk. No trust. Silent. *You can't make me.* You also saw a therapist, a man named Pete. He wore gray pants and sweater vests, and he was in a wheelchair. You and I had a session together with them, and I was encouraged to talk. To say how I felt. So I did.

When we left and walked down the sidewalk from the building to the car, you told me I was in trouble for telling those lies about you. You wanted to know why I would make up such horrible stories. I learned not to talk and not to tell.

When I got a little older, I ran away many times. One memorable time, I was gone for a few weeks, hiding in the upstairs attic bedroom of my friend Eva, where she slept with her sisters, Michelle, Yvette, Simone, and Clare. With so many young girls, I was able to slip in and out, and Eva brought me dinner. But eventually, the adults caught on. You came, and Eva's mother, and her father, and you, and Malcolm, and I talked.

I said you beat me. I said I wanted to stay there. I said I did not want to go home.

You said you loved me. You wanted me to come home. Things would be better.

I believed you. Or at least, I was persuaded that I couldn't stay there any longer and had to go home. I walked in the front door ahead of you. You kicked the door shut like you were a jiu-jitsu master, your leg jerking out sideways to whack the door shut. And then you whirled on me with your fists.

Lesson: Don't talk. Don't tell.

Message: You're a liar. Why do you betray your mother like that? She loves you.

Oh, Mom. Things were hard.

I love you,

Kim

*The couple on the left is Kim's Great Aunt Jewel and her husband.
On the right is Kim's Grandma and Grandpa.*

25

The Beatings

Dear Mom,

You beat me. A lot.

Your father beat your mother often (one time it was in the street after the movies with her sister and brother-in-law standing by). Your father beat you often (one time it was when you were two and you almost died from his beating). Your father beat your brother (one time it was with a shovel when he was eighteen).

Beating was a thing. An out-of-control thing.

The time came when you beat me.

A slap at ten.

A fist by fourteen.

Daily, just about, for many years.

We were in full-out war, and I resisted you in a variety of ways.

I punished you by going from straight-A student to flunking out.

I used words, telling you that you were out of control and couldn't do any better than to hit me.

I wouldn't let you tell me what to do.

The more I fought, the more you hit, and the more you hit, the more I escalated.

There was lots of screaming.

Alarm-the-neighbors screaming.

And shame. Lots and lots of shame. You called me:

Slut

Selfish

Whore

And spoke long strings of intellectual vitriol peppered with mocking put-downs.

You gave me a relentless, perpetual beatdown.

I'm not sure I've survived it. I am certain you didn't survive your childhood violence intact. I felt clear, even during the years of beatings, that you had promised yourself you would never do this to your children, but you kept losing control, over and over. Out of control.

Here's the thing. I know you are the parent who tried to show up. And, I know my dad was an alcoholic and sexually inappropriate, emotionally shut down, full-of-shame person. My options were fucked up, and yours weren't great either.

You are the perpetrator. You are the victim. You are the caregiver. You needed care. It is intergenerational. I know. I am so sad for the child you were, the part of you that lived inside and collapsed in your own helplessness many times, and who, when you came to the end of your life, rejected me. Maybe you meant to do that. Maybe you thought we'd have more chances. We didn't.

It's not about forgiving you or blaming you. It's about coming to peace with you.

I love you, Mom.

No more war.

Kim

26

———

Both Are True

Dear Mom,

Here's a fact: Our home was chaotic. At some point, all of it must have become too much for you. Our home became overrun with mice. Meredith even woke up in the middle of the night with mice running across her face.

So many obligations and activities were happening simultaneously: the anti-war movement, your studies in physics and geophysics, your work to raise two daughters, your Free Church marriage to Malcolm, and your efforts toward collective living and cooperative buying. Our house had a crazy, frenetic feel to it. And it was wildly exciting.

We used to get up at dawn to go protest at the Navy Base in Alameda. Then, at one point, the USS *Coral Sea* was docked there, and many sailors who resisted the war went AWOL. Four of them came to live with us. They stayed in our attic, with plywood laid down to make it habitable on top of the insulation and two-by-fours that previously comprised the floor. Hiding there, these four young soldiers told us they had been lied to. They went to war as patriots and then saw horrors and felt they could not support the U.S. war in Vietnam. So they jumped ship.

Anti-war posters in Kim's childhood bedroom.

And, in this case, hid in our attic. They were there for a long time—since I was about eleven years old, my gauge on time isn't likely to be that good. But one thing I know is that they stayed there long enough to make catching all the mice their entertainment. And then they put them in a glass container and began to tame and train the mice. I realize that must be an exaggeration; they couldn't have caught *all* the mice. But they did catch some. I remember that. And after they left, no more mice.

To sum up our home: Horrible. Mice. Neglect. Wonderful. Exciting. Adventure.

> I love you, Mom.
> Kim

Grandpa with a cat and a shotgun.

27

Beatrix Potter

Dear Mom,

I am in France at the moment. Last night as I drove out to the farmhouse/inn where I am lodging, I had the thought to drive slowly because animals might be out on the road. Sure enough, when I got to the driveway at the bottom of the hill, there was a raccoon crossing the road and caught in my headlights. A little smaller, longer, leaner, and lower to the ground than the fat city raccoons of Philadelphia (where I frequently saw them going through the trash), this little critter hustled out of my way with his ringed tail and pointy nose.

Tonight, as I came in, I thought again about animals and the road, but it is a misty, rainy night, and that thought was quickly followed by the idea that I have no need to worry—animals will be snug in their dens this wet night. Suddenly, I had a memory of Beatrix Potter, and I could see the little collection of stories tucked into their cardboard sleeve, their pastel colors, and I could feel the shared experience of loving them. This brought me memories of porcelain figures from Denmark, probably not related to Beatrix Potter, but of the same ilk: sweetness, innocence, a belief in magic, and beauty.

You gave us Beatrix Potter, Hans Christian Andersen (ah, there's the tie-in to Denmark and porcelain figures), and a love for animals. When you died, you had five cats: rescue, part feral, roam the house, hang out in the trees, fully anthropomorphized (by you) cats. And your brother found homes for every one of them. Not because of a particular fondness for cats but out of a very definite love for you. I'm so glad.

Mystical, beautiful, magical creatures were a part of your vocabulary in childlike ways. It's a miracle that any of that enchantment survived inside of you, as I know how much brutality you experienced as a child. But some little-kid self made it through intact—fragile and, perhaps, feral, but really truly there.

As I write this, I am remembering that your father, the same father with the violent temper, also had this childlike magic with creatures. He tamed crows and helped them heal broken wings, and he loved dogs who were mutts and called them his made-up word "hapertanians." He had a sort of gentleness in this regard. This is odd in contrast to the other parts of his personality, but maybe his little-boy self also had a place inside of him. I heard that his father was known as the meanest man in town—so bad things probably happened to your dad too. Thank you, Mom.

I love you,

Kim

28

The Ideal Job

Dear Mom,

I am laughing as I remember your professional advice to me circa 1987. You suggested I should get a job with the post office. Reliable, good benefits, retirement. You shared that your long-term partner had called me "a waste of a good brain." About a year later, I called you from the job I did have, a temp job as an admin that had turned permanent, about $11 an hour, and I told you I needed to go into treatment for drug and alcohol addiction. I'd been clean and sober a little over a week, and I was falling to pieces. You told me not to quit my job, no matter what, and to take some Bufferin. You said Bufferin was good for stress. I said that this was bigger than Bufferin.

I called you because you were about to co-sign a consolidation loan so I could get out of debt, and I didn't want you to sign without knowing my condition. I know you were worried about me. And your suggestion that I work at the post office was a gift of sorts. In that moment of listening to you tell me what I was capable of and how you felt about me, I knew that I had a different opinion of myself. For the first time in my life, I did not accept your version of me. I knew better. I was more than that. I

Kim at her desk job during a time when Bufferin was suggested as a cure for her early-stage recovery challenges.

had been working to find some self-esteem and self-love, and while I had a very long way to go, that tiny inkling that you were wrong was the sliver of light that came from self-knowledge, and it was enough to help me keep working to put myself on track. And then there's the evidence that you thought more was possible; after all, you were co-signing that loan.

We messed up, big time. We loved each other, and we really hurt each other a lot. I know you were proud of me as I progressed. I think you'd really groove off the things I do now.

I love you, Mom.
Kim

Mom in a school photo.

Mom as a professor.

29

Pontificating Professor

Dear Mom,

Not that long ago, I was in a work situation where my colleague was publicly rude to me. I was offended, did not understand, and retreated to the side of the room. My boss came over to me as I looked out the window at the New Orleans landscape, and she said, "You know, sometimes you come across like a pontificating professor."

Well, I had to laugh. Guess where I got that? A slightly professorial tone, perhaps even some condescension, and actual knowledge blended into an off-putting presence, well-intentioned but not well-received. That certainly can be me. And it definitely was you.

When my boss said that to me, it punctured my inflated indignation and brought me humor and a recognition that this was something I could change. Not everyone needs the benefit of our wisdom, Mom. Go figure!

Lots of love,

Kim

Meredith (right) hands Kim a flower.

30

Flower Children

Dear Mom,

I think it is fair to say that we were actual flower children. Me and Meredith. Forget digital native, we were flower children come to San Francisco, and we really did put flowers in our hair. You took us to Haight-Ashbury, we had fish and chips wrapped in newspaper and soaked in vinegar, people did the whole "greet and hug strangers on the street" thing and gifted us with actual love beads, and we sat in Golden Gate Park and made daisy chains and put them on our heads. We wore lots of tie-dye and shopped gleefully at the Goodwill and the Army/Navy Surplus store.

Your father would come to town and drive down the street, pointing out the hippies. It was a marvel to him; a life for us. Your brother Jerry was a captain in the Air National Guard. We put flowers in the bayonets of the National Guard when they occupied the Berkeley campus. Uncle Jerry would visit, and you two would have long discussions about right and left and who stood where. Family first. Politics second.

The fact that you left your small town and went on this grand adventure is a miracle. From my front row seat, the revolution became a part of who I am. For life. Thank you, Mom.

> I love you,
> Kim

31

Arrested

Dear Mom,

I remember when you were shot by the Berkeley police on Telegraph Avenue in the People's Park protest. You were part of a group that ended up suing the police for that. When I was going through your papers, I found the court letter with the disposition of the case. They had used rubber bullets, not flesh-penetrating, but left you with big bruises on the back of your thighs. You were arrested more than once and taken to Santa Rita Jail. I remember hushed voices in the middle of the night, soothing Meredith and me in our bunk beds. We were aware that you were in jail and that other adults were taking care of us and looking after you.

I think you would want to be remembered for your resistance to power. That you were part of the movement. You moved to Berkeley, and you joined the movement. You protested, and we joined you. We marched, we made silkscreen posters in basements on the U.C. Campus, we hated the "pigs" and the "establishment," we fell asleep at Marxist study groups, we watched the Red Detachment

Meredith and Mom at a Marxist study group.

Photo of an image on paper from the Red Detachment of Women. The print on the paper (not pictured) is in Chinese.

of Women ballet in Chinatown, and we believed we could disrupt the machine. We would not be cogs in the wheel of injustice. Fight the power! Thank you, Mom.

I love you,
Kim

Steven and Kim at their wedding in 1986.

32

You and Me and Black People

Dear Mom,

When we moved to Berkeley, you hired Thelma, a woman who came on Wednesdays to clean the house. It was the one day a week when someone was at home when Meredith and I got home from school. She would give us a dollar to walk to the Co-op Grocery Store and buy a half-dozen cinnamon rolls. We loved those cinnamon rolls. We loved Thelma. Thelma was African American and married to Alphonso. Because I was a child, somehow, I didn't learn their last names. Alphonso loaded trucks. He died young of a heart attack while loading a box of nails onto a truck. Too much weight.

You had a free magazine subscription offer, so you subscribed to *Jet* magazine for Thelma. This was my introduction to Black culture. Thelma's nurturing and *Jet* magazine. I read it every week.

Soon after, I was in the first wave of bussing to integrate the schools. And, at the same time, Nyambura and her boyfriend Bill moved in next door. They were friends of yours and Malcolm's, and she introduced me to African culture by way of dance, music, food, and parties almost every weekend. She became my Auntie Nyambura and my first dance instructor. Not because I took dance lessons from her, but because living next door to her was to be in her house and to learn to dance. She danced. I danced.

At school in the second year of integration, when I was in fifth grade, my teacher Jim started a Friday afternoon dance party to help the kids get along. I learned the funky chicken and the four corners, and the music of The Temptations, The Jackson 5, and The 5th Dimension. Records played on a small record player in a box with buckles that held the top on when it wasn't playing. Portable for that time. My first boyfriend, Al, was African American. He played drums on his desk.

In my family, this was a big problem, this Black boyfriend. Aunt Jean told "Grandpa" that "Kim had a Black boyfriend." This led to outrageous fights and me being called a White "N....." and a traitor to my race. Grandpa would drive me past bus stops with Black people at them, and he talked about lazy Black people and Cadillacs being purchased instead of money being well spent. He would say things like, "If there were a war against the 'N.....s,' I'd be the first one to get a gun." My father, also incensed, talked about mixed-race children[1] as being mentally retarded, an aberration. It was not good. It would be good if more White Americans acknowledged this hateful thinking passed on through our elders. This garbage has to be unlearned. Back then, you blamed Aunt Jean for being resentful enough against you to tell the

---

1 I am using the derogatory language of the time intentionally, because ugly is ugly. Today we would say differently abled —which would not in fact eliminate the perverted and bigoted perspective my father had.

family about me—winning points. You did not want to rock the boat. I got in big fights with everyone. I stuck to my convictions. Angry. Confused. Determined.

Al broke up with me in the hallway after school because his friends made fun of him for "going with a white girl."

Dancing made sense to me. I began flinging myself around at your parties, playing Jimi Hendrix, Big Brother and the Holding Company with Janis Joplin, and Santana. I took my role as entertainment seriously, and you gave me the stage.

I thrived on rhythm and felt at home with African American culture, and outside of the family's virulent box of racism, you encouraged this openness. You gave me a lot of room. Toni moved in next door, a woman with Louisiana family roots, and she had a baby boy, Chris, who became my dearest of beloved friends. I babysat him from birth until he was about nine, and Toni became another surrogate maternal figure for me. She cooked, and I learned how to make grits and jambalaya and how to get the "witch" out of okra. Saturday mornings were for *Soul Train* at her house. She played "Mr. Big Stuff" super loud on the record player because her husband was a jerk and she was in the middle of a divorce. She talked loud, laughed loud, and said outrageous things. She taught me how to wear make-up and gave me a couch to sleep on when things were too hard at home.

At age ten, I asked the Black Panthers if I could join them at their table out in front of the grocery store.

Then I became a bit older, like fourteen, and all my friends at Holy Names High School were young Black girls, and the nuns called you, and we had a meeting about my hanging out with people who seemed unsuitable. Well, things changed. You agreed with the nuns that I needed new friends. I was outraged. I wrote a very long poem in red ink about what I perceived as your racism, your father's racism, an inheritance. I had already read George Jackson, Bobby Seale, and Eldridge Cleaver. By that time, I was on to learning about the Harlem Renaissance and Marcus Garvey, and reading Richard Wright, Frantz Fanon, and the autobiography of Malcolm X. I could not be told what to do. At that same time, you hired a woman named Mrs. Pear to be home when Meredith and I got there. A small, round White woman with short, curly hair, she didn't last long. She left a note when she quit, saying I was incorrigible and hedonistic, and I listened to jungle music—she was out of there. This actually made you laugh. Meredith and I were happy to see her go.

When I married a Black man, you said it had to be a secret from your father. I insisted I would tell him. I was adamant that I would not shame my husband by denying him. My husband intervened with my plan, saying, "Go along to get along." And, he told me he was afraid. Afraid that angry White men would hurt him. In the seven years we were together, I learned a lot about the back-of-the-neck awareness of danger that never leaves a Black man. Especially one with a White woman as a partner. I told my father instead. He basically ignored this information except to say, "Don't bring any of those people over here." When I became seriously involved with a Black woman years later, he stopped speaking to me permanently. Homophobia turned out to be even stronger than incipient racism.

Over the course of our experiences with Black people, you tried to tell me that Black culture was not suitable for me. Hoop earrings were for Black girls, not me. Black vernacular was okay for the neighbor Toni but not appropriate for me to use. There was this weird, convoluted message about being open and caring about equality and yet not "mixing." I think you were somewhere on the spectrum between trying to avoid cultural appropriation, a more contemporary idea, and not mixing outside of our own race, a more regressive idea. Your small-town life and your Berkeley life didn't quite prepare you for a daughter who identified with the cultures of the African diaspora. YET, without you, I would never have known Thelma, or read the books I read, or been Nyambura's little shadow.

Thank you for all that you let me explore.

I love you, Mom.
Kim

33

Breathtaking Arrogance

Dear Mom,

Today I am writing to share with you about what I call my breathtaking arrogance. I began to think about this last October when I was in France; specifically, I was in Auch for the Circa Festival. I went to hear a conversation with a choreographer who was chosen to work with a company I greatly admire. As he began to talk about his process, I could hear the dialogue in my own brain saying, *I could do that.* It makes me laugh and pause to reflect. How on earth is it that I seem to think that his years of study and practice are inconsequential compared to my hubris? How is it that I think I can do anything without regard for the work, the effort, and the time it takes to become accomplished at something? How is it that I think I am entitled, that I deserve, whatever it is that I choose? This mindset is alarming when it presents itself.

There are ways that the mindset is helpful in that it has plunged me forward into a series of events that lead to learning and new adventures, often with lots of alarming challenges and setbacks, but still forward motion. I am not so much referring to the positive side of risk-taking that can come about from this quality. I am looking at the shadow side—the part where I simply think that I can, I must, I will be seen and appreciated. The this-requires-no-effort, I-can-do-it, and even I-deserve-it side of this attitude. The reflection of the energy that my father resented in you and then attributed to me when he said, "You are just like your mother. You think you're too good for me." That quality. The part where your father would refer to people as having "bad blood." The choices our family can make to brush others aside and put ourselves forward. The choices I make to put myself forward. That kind of arrogance is breathtaking.

That is where unearned privilege lives. In that energy.

I can easily recall your quality of this sort, the dismissiveness you expressed when anyone was not your intellectual equal, and the way you talked about others, their work, and their effort as inferior. The way you could easily refer to someone as an idiot. A fool. The way you could push ahead in a line.

This, too, is me. When I went to Greece with my friend, I had the privilege of airline miles to put me in a shorter line, and my friend did not. I took the privilege and let my friend stand in the longer line. That is fucking breathtakingly arrogant.

I—for sure—do not blame you for this quality in me. I'm simply sharing it as I reflect on how it plays out. It's something to look at as I shift away from entitlement and toward generosity of spirit.

I love you, Mom.
Kim

34

The Other Side of Chile

Dear Mom,

So much is painful. So much is true. So much was taken from me in the blazing nature of the wounds inflicted on me in Chile when I was eight. Still, not every truth is painful. In Chile, in 1968, I learned about music, maracas, and all-night parties with people young and old singing and dancing. I found out that the music of the Andes was different than the Mariachi music of home. Everyone played an instrument, everyone knew a song, and when kids got ready to drop in exhaustion, mattresses were thrown down on the floor for children to sleep on as the parties continued all night before we children were carried through dawn-lit streets to home and to bed.

In Chile, we lived in a big house with Margarita there to care for us while you and your deeply problematic male companion George were at the university. Margarita spoke no English, and Meredith and I, six and eight years old, spoke no Spanish. Still, we trundled off to the Spanish-speaking-only school, Nido de Aguilas, which involved a hair-raising bus ride on windy mountain roads (hence the name, which means "eagle's nest") and where the threat of having our mouths washed out with soap

Kim, Margarita, and Meredith.

if we spoke any English kept us in line. When we got home, there was Margarita. We kept a Spanish/English dictionary on top of the refrigerator, and we made it work. She would fry flour in hot oil on the stovetop and then cover it with powdered sugar—delicious. *The Three Stooges* were on the black-and-white television in the living room as the only program in English.

We were good during those afternoons with Margarita. She took care of us with love, warmth, and laughter, and we were safe. There was a swimming pool, three dogs—a collie, a boxer, and one I cannot recall—plus seven Japanese chickens and many, many trees. At one point during this time in Chile, we took a trip all the way to the southern tip, traveling by car for many days. We stopped along the way at a ranch and rode horses through the manzanita (I fell off). We ended up near a lake very far south where the roads were not paved. We stayed at a motel and accidentally started a fire by putting a scarf over a lamp to dim the light. Nothing catastrophic, just a memory. I still have a small blue hand-beaded bracelet from that trip.

When you left George by running, hiding, and getting to Peru with the help of friends, we still had good experiences while we waited in a Lima hotel for funds to be wired by your father to get us the rest of the way home. We went and saw llamas with their long tongues and woolly fur. We got ponchos of soft alpaca and saw those animals too. We got multicolored woven hats that raised to a soft round peak on our heads and had flaps to cover our ears. We were treated kindly by the hotel staff.

There was suffering in Chile. My own suffering and the deep poverty of the family that lived in a cardboard and tin shack just through a barbed-wire fence on the other side of the property where we stayed. I still have a scar on my leg from that barbed wire. We learned about new places and connecting with people. We made it home.

And then, in 1973, when Salvador Allende's government was overthrown with the assistance of the CIA, we had a connection to that place. We had a feeling of connection to the people there, to what was happening. We had friends in Chile, and we feared for their lives. That other September 11th, when soldiers in boots marched through the presidential palace and trampled on top of people, when democratic students were thrown from helicopters, and when people were rounded up and tortured, kept in the central stadium, and shot and killed. We grieved Victor Jara, who had played the music of the revolution before his fingers were brutally smashed as he was tortured and then killed. We were there for the founding of La Pena Cultural Center in Berkeley, and you wondered out loud if you should smuggle weapons to aid the students, your friends from your time at the university there.

So much came from all the choices you made, and I am the recipient of the learning, the experiences, the connections, and the meanings that arise from the road we traveled. You instilled in me a sense of the people's revolution, social justice, and the right to protest. It's true you gave me a big world.

Thank you, Mom.

I love you,
Kim

35

—

France

Dear Mom,

I am not sure where your love of France came from. Some romantic notion about Europe, perhaps a residue of your European honeymoon, maybe something inherited from your mother, possibly an influence from your friend Michelle, or just a general association with European culture that got all bundled up into something known as France. What I do know is that later in life, you fulfilled your dream of France by taking a vacation in the south with the lavender fields, the stone cottages, the sunflowers, and even the painting classes. You did not like it. You came home and told me you were lonely.

I'm sorry for that.

> I love you, Mom.
> And, I really love France.
> Kim

VALA BOVIE

Madam Vala Bovie's School of Dance brochure.

36

Pink Tutus

Dear Mom,

It must have been very strange to you to have me as a daughter. You struggled to make a way in the world and overcome so much patriarchal oppression. Getting yourself to Berkeley and enrolled in the university, with two daughters, took a force of will that is hard to imagine. Here I come, and I want to take ballet. I read a biography of Anna Pavlova, and I was enamored of dance, I learned that even five years old isn't too young to start, and that, in fact, it might be too late after, and I was enraptured. I must take ballet.

I found Madam Vala Bovie's School of Dance. I begged for ballet lessons. I wanted it all—pink leotards, tutus, ballet shoes. You, a newly hatched feminist, actually went to bra-burning events. You were embracing science, and you were a student. Your values and your budget were not aligned with my balletic aspirations. I can only imagine how you felt; you fought to overcome obstacles and the required gender structures for little girls, and I just wanted to be a ballerina.

I'm finally old enough to mostly let go of that ballet dream thing, even if it still makes me a little wistful to

Kim dancing and singing in a pink skirt (not exactly a tutu).

have romantic notions of the life of a ballerina. It is a pretty powerful archetype. I got the best dance possible through the friends and neighbors who lived movement as an intrinsic part of life, of culture, and of community, and that knowledge has made my life a million times richer. I appreciate you, Mom.

I love you,
Kim

37

———

Knees

Dear Mom,

My knees are sore now. Not all the time, but certainly a feeling that I pay attention to. I can be seen (but thankfully not) sitting down on lower toilet seats with my arms extended like a gymnast coming in for a perfect landing, counterbalancing my weight to reduce the pressure on my knees. I remember this slow deterioration of your knees, your father's knees, and now gradually mine. This same story applies to my sister, and your sister, and your brother. Knees challenged by shin bones with a curvature that torques the whole thing. You told me when you learned this about your own anatomy.

This year, a physical therapist told me the same thing, and I was instructed to order sole inserts for my shoes. Arch support. Not super glamorous. I know that I am aging because when I walked down to the beach at Half Moon Bay recently, I took my time and found careful placement for my feet. No more the joy of nimble footing; replaced, instead, by caution for my knees. Yoga, weight training, and acupuncture all help. Yet, the rolling gait of a sailor as your father compensated for his knees, and the hitch in your walk as you headed toward your car, are familiar motions that now insert themselves into my movement from time to time as well. Meredith told me that when you were weakened by radiation treatment, you had difficulty sitting on the toilet, and a sort of seat belt was constructed for extra assistance to help you be there with no support from your knees or your limbs. This feels tragic.

I love you, Mom.
Kim

38

Leaving Dad

Dear Mom,

Okay. So. Once upon a time. You lived in a little house in a town called Clovis, on Clovis Avenue. You had two friends named Gail and Coke. Gail had three children, Kate, Terry, and Ross, and Coke had two girls, Joelle and Elise. You had me and Meredith. You would take turns having the kids all together at each other's houses, or perhaps we'd all go to the Dairy Freeze for chocolate-dipped soft serve ice cream cones. Hot, hot San Joaquin Valley summers, running through the sprinkler, swimming in an irrigation ditch, and powwows[2] organized by the women's club with horses and cake competitions. You had a hand-cranked meat grinder for making hamburgers, and you served canned peas and wore your hair in a sort of bouffant do.

I was too young to understand or know that Dad played cards, played baseball, drank beer, and came home drunk. I didn't know how you had yearned for

---

2 Author's note: I realize that the use of the word *powwow* to refer to a social get-together in contexts that are not related to Indigenous Americans is considered an offensive cultural appropriation. In this letter to my mother, I used the word in a way that the women's club had used it during those years.

Dad as a little boy.

college and education, how you enrolled as an art major at Fresno State University and played French horn in the symphony. You wanted more. You wanted different.

After high school, you had been accepted to Stanford University but not allowed to go. Your father said that girls don't leave small towns to go to college. Your mother could not have fought that battle, despite her fierce advocacy for education, because she was terrorized by beatings at the hand of her husband. Your father.

Instead you got a job at the airport the summer after high school, announcing flight departures and arrivals. Dad worked for United Airlines. You met. You married. You left your father's house for my father's house, and it was only a marginal improvement. A transitional stage of sorts. One that included two babies and, I think, an effort to make it work.

It didn't work. His drunkenness, his lack of interest in the life intellectual, his sublimated shame that came out sideways in sexual bullying and inappropriate transgressions in my bedroom at night, where my fear of his incursions made for restless nights and bad dreams.

And one night, he threatened you with a gun. I guess everyone has a trip wire. A break point. That was yours. What I remember is you waking me up, wrapping Meredith in a bundle of blanket, and having us curl up on the floor of the car in the backseat. Hide. Quiet. Drive without headlights. Go home. Go back to your mother's house. She was comfort and safety. Later that night, Dad came. We were in the bedroom down the hall with twin beds and light slipping in the windows from the security light in the yard. Dad was at the back door. Banging. Yelling. And eventually, the soft voice of Grandma, speaking to him. He was sobbing. Remorseful. We did not go with him. By the time we went back to that little ranch house on Clovis Avenue, he was gone. Living in a "Bonadelle home" in Fresno. He moved on and married again but always mourned you.

Uncle Jerry moved in for a year, and he brought jumping on beds and dancing to Diana Ross and The Supremes. I learned the monkey, the jerk, the stroll, and the Freddie. You hung out at the one café, with black-and-white checked tiles on the floor, where people drank espresso and played chess, near Fresno State. You packed a U-Haul, put your things and a decorated Christmas tree in the back, and off we went to Berkeley.

Free. Saved. New. Alive. 1966. Thank you, Mom.

I love you,
Kim

39

Baggage

Dear Mom,

Last week, in Luxembourg, I walked to the train station on Sunday to get the lay of the land. I was going to be leaving from Luxembourg to Paris on Monday with colleagues from work, and I wanted to know how far I would have to walk, where the platform was, and how to exchange my ticket for a later train to suit the schedule that my coworkers had modified.

On my way there, I was thinking about the suitcases I had with me on the trip (one small and one slightly larger than medium), their weight, and what it would take to get them through the streets, up and down stairs, and onto the train. In particular, I was imagining how I would do that without asking any of the three men I would be traveling with to help me. They would be coming from Paris, no luggage in tow, and I wanted to be maintenance-free for them. No trouble at all. This led me to think about a coworker I have and how, when traveling in Europe with her, I've observed her approach to lugging a very large suitcase around. She unabashedly looks for strong young men, flatters them enormously, and asks them for help followed by profuse praise as she thanks them afterward.

Classic Mom in the 1960s.

I had to wonder what prevents me from using that approach. What keeps me from turning toward the need for assistance and then seeking help? I avoid asking for help if at all possible and can even become indignant at the suggestion that I cannot manage on my own. These thoughts went through my mind as I traversed the gray and uneven sidewalk, the lackluster misty day, the gentle bustle of the city, and the path unfolding before me that I would need to navigate the following day.

And here is the answer. It is twofold. I think some of my impulse to be independent and not rely on anyone for help has its roots in early feminism. I recall the shift—the adamant refusal to allow a man to open a door, light a cigarette, or in this case, lift your luggage. *I am woman, hear me roar. I can do it.* This was especially present for you as you sorted through how to be a scientist in a man's world. I watched you suit up and show up for field work in a turtleneck, down vest, jeans, and hiking boots for long hours in the lab, not hindered by children or showing any weakness, and eschewing any form of femininity as a matter of contempt.

This, I think, is tied to my refusal to acknowledge the need for help; those long years of you in the laboratory taught me to need nothing. To ask for nothing. That any request from your children was overwhelming and unmanageable, and ultimately, my sense of myself was that I was a burden to you. If I need something, I will become expendable. Better to manage on my own. Don't worry, Mom, I am okay. I can handle it. I can lug my own baggage.

I love you,
Kim

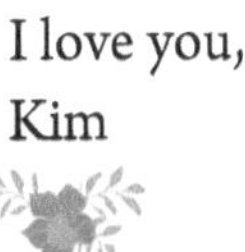

Mom and Malcolm at their wedding.

40

———

Men

Dear Mom,

We have a complicated history, you and me, when it comes to men. Really, I feel like I should put the word in capital letters: MEN. Damn. Where do I even start?

When we moved to Berkeley, you had a series of lovers. Some were just a little bit gross (to a kid) like Frank, who had big sloppy kisses, glasses, and unruly hair, a philosophy professor who seemingly helped you get the liftoff you needed to leave Clovis. Or Mark, who had a very long ding dong and believed in walking around nude and saying good morning to me and Meredith when we were still in our bunk beds. I can still see that thing. Some were handsome and charming and fun like Lou the glassblower and sculptor or Pierre the French man with a Triumph, a TR6 that we jetted around in and got forbidden food from McDonald's. Or the one devastatingly violent man, George, who was a sadist and the one we went to Chile with. And then Malcolm, who tried to parent but also wanted to be a pal, and who ultimately had prurient feelings he professed when I was eighteen. With all those men, I would run to open your car door or light your cigarette before they could (men still did that in those days)—me valiantly trying in some way to court you myself, to claim you, to make you mine. I would interrupt your sex life while I lay in my bed with a tenseness in my body, alert to the sounds that would start, and then I would cry out for you, wanting the sounds to stop.

You called me melodramatica hysterica.

When you married Malcolm, you made us all dresses from raw fabric, simple and lovely. Later, when I saw a picture of myself with Uncle Jerry, leaning against him, I thought I looked great! You said I looked like a prostitute, a street walker. At ten.

When I was younger, you had lots of student parties, and I would play chess, ask precocious questions about math and science, or fling my body around in space to the music of the time. When I got older, you held these same parties, and when I practiced this same behavior, you became furious. As my sexuality presented, your communication to me became more and more violent.

I can feel it in my body now. A grave sadness. You blamed me. You felt a sort of twisted competitiveness with me. I felt a romantic attachment to you. I wanted you all to myself. I loved you. The more violent you became toward me, the more I provoked you, the wilder I became in my adolescent sexuality, and the more intensely we fought. You beat me. You screamed at me. You shoved me into the bathroom and closed the door so I had to sit in that small, one-toilet room. You frequently, and eventually permanently, sent me away. You could not tolerate me. I became intensely afraid of you.

I know you were hurt. I want to send you love and solidarity now. Women who were violently abused are injured, and you were injured early and often. Loving you was confusing.

I love you, Mom.
Kim

Meredith and Kim are wearing homemade dresses for the Free Church wedding of Mom and Malcolm and are pictured here with their cousin and Uncle Jerry.

*Kim, Meredith, and Mom around the time
that Kim attended Bay High School.*

41

———

Age-Appropriate

Dear Mom,

One thing you got super twisted was intellectual capability and emotional maturity. I was ten when you sent me on a backpacking trip where the age of admission was supposed to be thirteen. Backpacking in the high Sierra. With teenagers and young adults. Somehow, the fact that I'd read Shakespeare and Hermann Hesse and D.H. Lawrence meant I was suited for friends who were older than me. True enough, I was out of step with kids my own age. Reading beyond their level and using big words was not a way to fit in. That did not improve when I was around older kids. I was excruciatingly self-conscious. I was miserable. The pack was so heavy, and I was marching up the mountain paths grudgingly, and no one wanted to talk to me other than the conscientious hike guides who were there to lead us on. I can recall that there were glorious moments, and given that I haven't been backpacking since, those memories of alpine meadows, sliding down a summer snowcap, and drinking the purest sweetest water from my tin cup that swung from a hook on my belt will have to serve for a lifetime. I cannot imagine exactly what you were thinking. I was too ashamed to take off my clothes in front of the other kids, so I wore my bathing suit bottom for the whole trip (which was three weeks)—never putting on fresh underwear. Not a good plan. Midway through the trip, I was so unhappy that I stood on a big granite boulder and tried to figure out how to jump off and break my arm so I could go home. At a waypoint when we were near a campground, I pleaded with a woman to take me home. She did. When I got there, you sent me back!

In that same era, one night you got a call from your friends Doron and Yael. They had begun participating in couples swapping—called swingers at the time—and were at a party where the beverages had been spiked with acid and they were having a very bad trip. Convinced that the other people at the party were out to get them, they desperately wanted to leave but were too scared to drive. You woke me up to go get them with you. Somewhere up on the winding road of the Arlington, we found them shivering under a dark tree and took them to their home. Once there, Doron became agitated and began yelling. Yael became hysterical and began crying. We split up— you to calm down Doron in the kitchen, and me to sit with Yael in the living room. She sobbed and began to get even more distressed, pleading with me to promise her that I would never take acid. She was getting more and more hysterical until I swore I would never ever take acid. This turned out well for me, as later when I became a drug addict and took lots of things, I could never bring myself to break that particular promise, which probably kept me from permanently frying my brain.

Not dismayed by this experience and apparently not taking in any feedback about how I felt about being forced into these experiences I was too young to handle, a few years later when I was twelve, you enrolled me in Bay High School. A new experiment in learning located on 6th and Gilman, a "free school" in a warehouse with candle-dipping, bread kneading, ceramics, and a choose-your-own-adventure approach to the rest. Kids wore bell-bottoms and poison rings with tabs of acid in them, and lots of making out was happening. We took trips to the Russian River, where we all skinny-dipped, and there were big piles of late-night "loving" that completely blew my mind. I had to get in the river with my bathing suit on and then throw it to the riverbank—too shy to walk around unclothed. The girls had breasts and pubic hair. I did not. And the boys had pubic hair too! I was out of my depth for sure.

This was in the days of rap sessions, and Gestalt therapy had just moved in the direction of primal screaming. One day, I was in a primal screaming session where a curly-haired, red-headed guy named Michael was screaming out his pain. We were all around him to lend support. In the middle of his very major release, he stopped, sat up on the bed, and looked over at me. He said he didn't feel I was present with him; I was ruining the vibe. I was asked to leave. *Sheesh.* I called Malcolm, my stepfather, to come get me. Another time, in our creative writing class, which took place on Sunday evenings at the teacher's house, we were all sitting in a circle when one of the students, Darcy, asked if she could take a bath. She was excited by the claw-footed bathtub. And then, the instructor said he would join her! And we were all invited into the bathroom to watch—as a creative writing exercise to witness, and then we could write about it. *Double sheesh!*

There I was, still twelve years old, watching this woman (eighteen, by the way) and this instructor (pretty young himself with dark curly hair and a beard) splash around in the tub, soap up, and slip-slide around on each other. When he stood up, he dropped the towel and it hung on his erection. This time, no one had to tell me that I wasn't getting the vibe. I left and called Malcolm, again, to come get me. Later, I was considered a social outcast because I talked about this, and it turned out Darcy was involved with Chas, who was living in my attic bedroom while I slept on a piece of foam in the living room—and Chas broke up with Darcy because I came home and talked about what I had seen. Bad me. *OMG.*

So many things that were out of step with my age. After that, I got to leave Bay High and have tutors, a geophysicist who was in school with you (and who had become a lover to one of your quasi-boyfriends/thesis advisor and had a baby out of wedlock, and he married someone else; lots of drama there) and her room-mate who was a sort-of out, but not quite, lesbian and English major. They taught me paleontology, geometry, Nathaniel Hawthorne's *The Scarlet Letter*, and how to bake apple rhubarb pie. There were also baths, but just me and the baby.

Really, as they say, you can't make this shit up.

I love you, Mom.
Kim

42

Children

Dear Mom,

When I am in a restaurant and children are there, or children arrive, I have a programmed and automatic response. *Oh. No. Children.* Fair enough. Children make noise. Children run around. Children are messy. Children are disruptive. Still, this is more your response than mine. All these years later, your immediate, automatic, and negative response to the presence of children is ingrained in me. I love children. Children, usually, totally dig me. I know how to vibe them without words. They're magic. They play games with me through their eyes. Surprise and delight. Shining knowledge beaming from their being. I love children.

Not you. This response you had to children in restaurants was not that different from your feelings about parenting. Those were explicitly shared. You were clear. Starting when I was about seven, you began talking about having children as a big mistake that you had made and that you hoped I would avoid. I remember being in your closet when we had a conversation about it. You had a purple knit bell-bottom two-piece pantsuit and a kaftan top and other cool things to wear in there; I liked

Dad and Mom, Kim and Meredith.

your closet, and this conversation was in the nature of a sharing conversation. You were feeling open and honest and confiding in me like a friend. Like a grown-up. "Don't have children. It will ruin your life."

Yikes! I was your kid.

I'm laughing as I write this, thinking about the feminism and the mothering and the good intent you had with that information. Information you repeated on the regular. And often, it was not shared in quite such a congenial way. Whichever way you shared it, it imprinted, and both my sister and I remember the message quite clearly: Having children is a mistake.

For me, when I was old enough to have children and foolish enough to conceive, meaning eighteen years old, I wanted very much to have babies. I got pregnant but did not stay pregnant. I had no support system, and I was very much in trouble.

All the years after that when I could have had babies, I did not. Inside of myself, I was deeply afraid I would damage children. I was afraid of the rage inside of me that might make me do harm. Real harm. I was afraid of the emotional world that lived inside of me and how I might not be able to make good choices. Nurturing choices. I really believed that if I had a child, I would hurt that child. So I did not.

In my early forties, I finally felt like I could safely give birth to, nurture, and raise a child. Still without a partner, and even still without much money, I tried to get pregnant by accident—also known as having unprotected sex with men too young to want to wear condoms. They weren't random guys; they were guys I was dating. It turns out that when I was in my forties, it was men in their twenties who found me attractive. That choice sort of contradicts the idea that I was mature enough to have children. It was a foolish venture. And, it didn't work. I ran to the clinic several times to see if I was pregnant when my period was late, and I became a bit of a laughingstock there because they assured me this menstrual irregularity was the onset of perimenopause, not a sign of life, a baby. All that urge to get pregnant, my body's urgency at its last-chance status of the likelihood of pregnancy, seized me for about two years. But, no baby.

Sometimes, I still daydream about carrying and birthing a child, bringing them up, and connecting in that way. I also register and acknowledge that your truth about children was a sensible one. Children are work. They are all-consuming. Having children can be a mistake if you are not equipped to raise them. You certainly tried to provide and to educate and to give me what I needed to succeed. You really didn't want children, you didn't know how to be available in a loving way, and you couldn't manage to recover from your own childhood.

In restaurants, I still have to remember that I enjoy children—and yes, they can be annoying.

I love you, Mom.
Kim

43

Tabu

Dear Mom,

Last night, I was thinking about Meredith and her new puppy, which is making her so happy, and it brought Tabu to mind. Remember when Meredith and her friend Ossie went to the Co-op Grocery Store to sit out front and try to give away the puppies that Ossie's German shepherd had given birth to? In those days, people would sit out front and give away kittens and puppies. Well, that day, they sat out front all day and didn't give away any puppies. In fact, someone else who had been trying to give away a puppy had given up, left the puppy in a shopping cart, and walked away. So the girls came back with an extra puppy instead of giving any away. Ossie's father, Amir, said, "No way." The extra puppy came home with Meredith. (I'm recognizing a trend here as I flash forward to more than fifteen years later when you and Meredith went to the pound for a dog and came home with two.) Anyway, back circa 1970, Meredith came home with this extra puppy.

Our rented home didn't allow dogs; the dog had to go. Only, we got attached. We think he was part Basenji because of his markings, his curly tail, and his inability to bark. That last part is quite helpful if you're trying to

Kim, Meredith, and Mom with Tabu.

hide the fact that you have a dog in a no-dogs-allowed rental. So, with lots of remonstrations that Meredith had to take care of the dog, you were not going to take care of the dog, and I had to help with the dog, and all those things that parents everywhere must say when kids want pets, he stayed. He was named Tabu, as in taboo, as in not allowed. Forbidden.

And then, what happened, which probably almost always happens in households where kids get dogs that they are supposed to take care of, Tabu became your dog. Which probably reflects how dogs find the person they are supposed to be with, because for sure, Tabu and you were meant to be. He went to the university with you every day, stayed long hours in the lab, and came home with you late at night. He was able to take the elevator by himself, somehow navigate between floors, go outside to walk himself, and return to you again. Many people told the story of their amazement to have the elevator doors open in the Earth Sciences Building and see Tabu walk out on his own and down the hall to the lab. He was quite well known by everyone. In fact, when you got your PhD, Tabu walked with you to get your diploma, and he was awarded an honorary degree. So much love, so much companionship. People don't give away dogs in front of grocery stores anymore, and dogs are rarely given the freedom to walk themselves in urban centers, but little girls and puppies still find each other, and moms are still the ones who end up with the loyal companions.

I love you, Mom.

Kim

Kim and Meredith on the back of the Chevy II.

44

————

White Cars

Dear Mom,

I have this weird phobia about white cars. I will not drive them. At car rental desks, I refuse white cars. Why? I don't know. Perhaps it has something to do with the white Ford Pinto that you were given by your father.

Before that, when we first moved to Berkeley, you had a Chevy II white convertible with a red interior. Someone ran a stop sign and plowed into you, and the car was totaled. We were sad. After that, we got your mother's green Chevy Impala, a gift from your father because Grandma had died and we had no car. Apparently, we were a Chevrolet family—although Grandpa drove a Cadillac—but Uncle Jerry had a Malibu Super Sport, another Chevrolet. In any case, that big green car was like a boat. We made fun of it, and I think you were embarrassed by it. It was huge. Eventually, when it was no longer functional, your father bought you another car, a white Pinto station wagon (apparently now we bought Fords). That car was functional, and you were disappointed by its lack of style. One day when I was about twelve, I jumped in it and my sister got in the front seat. You used to give us the keys to go start the car (warming up a car was apparently still a thing then), and I said to my sister, "Let's surprise Mom." I drove the car slowly around the block. It was funny afterward, but I think it scared you a lot at the time. The Pinto lasted a super long time until it died rusting out in your front driveway in Davenport. That car was the car you drove me to school in during ninth and tenth grades, where I would be delivered to the steps of the school, crying, as you had denigrated and hit me all the way to school. You had the ability to have one hand on the wheel and the other arm extending, fold in, aim out, fist, hit, face, me. Maybe that's why I don't like white cars.

When you finished school and gained some financial independence, you bought a Fiat X19. A tiny little jet of a car that had the top lifted out and then placed underneath the front hood. Your convertible. Your sports car. You loved driving with sharp edges and tight turns, and you were happy with the comparison to Mario Andretti. You loved that car. I got it when you moved on to a red Mazda Miata. The Fiat had 165,000 miles on it, and I drove it for a few more years.

I like to drive too. Like you, I stayed with a stick shift until just this year, preferring the control and the sensation of driving. You learned to drive a tractor by the time you were five. One day, you bounced off the tractor seat, and the back tire rolled right over you. Thanks to the soft soil and your still-childlike bones, you were fine. Your father lifted you up and ran sobbing all the way to the house with you in his arms.

Love, hate, control, cars, tears, joy, sharing, caring, all mixed up in our history together.

I love you, Mom.

Kim

45

Melanie

Dear Mom,

In 1994, I fell in love. Deeply. Smashingly. Breathtakingly smitten. With Melanie. While I had felt feelings and kissed a girl, a friend, at eleven years old, I knew even then to be afraid of the idea that I might be a lesbian. I don't recall any homophobia from you when I was young, but for sure, lesbians were on the list of things Dad talked about in the bigoted way things came out of his mouth. *Bull dykes. Can't get a man. Lesbian. Nobody wants to love them.* So I had fear, even as I had desire and curiosity.

I can look back now and see the friends I was in love with as distinct from the girls who were my friends as a young girl and woman. By my thirties, I was ready to find out. I tried going out to the G-Spot in San Francisco, to breakfast at the Brick Hut in Oakland, and generally showing up at known lesbian locations. I asked a lot of questions. I wasn't sure how I was going to test out this lesbian/bisexual self and find out more about who I was. I took a class on "Women and their Bodies," and the instructor was in her sixties, had been married, had children, and then came out. I asked her how she knew.

Melanie and Kim with Meredith on Meredith's wedding day.

What she did. When, how, what. She told me to try it and find out. *Damn.* How do I go about doing that?

And then I saw Melanie. She was onstage at an Oakland Youth Chorus (OYC) concert where I was interviewing to be the Managing Director, and I was struck by lightning, and immediately clear that she was my love. After the concert, I did not try to talk to her immediately but eventually said something to her. She asked if she knew me, and I said, "No, but you will." And I left. I began work at OYC, and thus followed a year of breathless anticipation, flirtation, and service to her. I would offer to drive her to her gigs, as she didn't like to drive, and for days after, I would be trembling inside. She was a wave of consciousness, a sound vibration, a reality that was meant to dawn inside of me. I told her that I felt her so deep inside my bones that my ancestors knew her. And one day, we kissed. At the Berkeley Rose Garden. After dark. After dinner. I didn't know where to put my hands. Breasts were exciting and confusing. We began. We loved. I believed we would spend the rest of our lives together.

I called you to share. You were appalled. I think you were scared. I was sad. I thought I was sharing with you the amazing and thrilling news that I had actually found love—that rare miracle. You said you were afraid I would lose my job, and I took it personally. I saw it as your homophobia. You saw it as being protective of me in an unforgiving society.

A year or so later, at my sister's wedding, you were rude to me and to Melanie. You wouldn't speak to us, and you talked about us to others. Meredith, in a rare burst of courage, stood up to you and everyone else, recognizing Melanie as my partner and including her. Even in the wedding photos. She loved Melanie too. Melanie helps scared people be brave. And she gives children safe places to be when they are with her. Meredith felt safe with Melanie. In a surprise turn of events, my rigid, racist, bigoted father was nice to her and to me. That day. After that day, he never spoke to me again. He saw it as Meredith's day, and he was not going to spoil it. But after that, he was through with me.

You, Mom, you came to tolerate Melanie's presence. Yet you still went to a family wedding where I was not invited because of homophobia, and you kept it a secret. So did Meredith. Our Great Aunt June in her eighties told me; she was so disappointed that I was excluded.

Year over year, Melanie witnessed the hurt, the rejection, and the experience I had of being around you. And then, one day, you changed your position. Your friend and neighbor had a daughter who had a woman lover. Then she broke up with that woman and married a man. And then, your friend said she missed the days when her daughter was with a woman. The woman had come over and helped to fix things. The woman had cared for her daughter in tangible, take-care-of-her ways. The woman had shared space and talked and listened. The man did not do these things. He watched sports. He did not help cook. He did not repair things. He seemed useless compared to the woman. And you—you heard these things and found that it was socially acceptable, and even cool, that your daughter was with a woman. And I think it spoke to your feminist heart. These words of women bonding and men not helping were a part of a narrative you responded to. With this social validation, you were ready to accept Melanie.

It was too late. After five years of loving Melanie and four years together, we broke up. It was a painful breakup. I did not see her again until a few years after you were gone, and I was struggling with your choice not to see me before you died. I remembered that Melanie would always tell me that she hated it when I visited you because I always came back hurt and a bit broken. I asked to see her so she could help me remember this dynamic. To help me understand, perhaps, a bit more about you and me, as she remembered us. She didn't say much. She said you were a brilliant asshole. Shocking and not typical language for her. She said more. I wish I could remember it all now. It was something along the lines of suggesting I live with more attention on those who do love me and let go of what cannot be repaired.

Oh, Mom, I want so much to be close to you.

I love you,
Kim

46

God and Church

Dear Mom,

When I was born, you were expected to baptize me. Or rather, have me baptized. This was not a willing choice on your part. It was a requirement. Your mother, a devout Methodist, played the church organ on Sunday, led the choir, and was a respected member of the church. Your husband's mother was a member of the Church of Christ, a super-strict sect that my father didn't participate in but rather felt shamed by until late in life when he returned to the church. There was no decision to make about baptism other than which church. You chose Episcopalian. In your estimation, it was the most liberal and had the most interesting rituals, and therefore, that was where I was baptized.

In truth, you were an atheist. Your departure from Clovis let you release the need to be conventional. I, for some reason, longed for God. You found the rituals of the church macabre, and when your mother died in 1969, you would not let Meredith and me attend the funeral. You felt it would be detrimental to us as children to witness the gathering at the church. Instead, we were with our father, who took us to Yosemite and said it was too bad our grandmother wasn't going to heaven. He said she was a good woman, but a Methodist. Wrong church. I walked to the local dairy farm and talked to the cows who gathered at the fence. It was January and the ground was muddy. The cows had big brown eyes and seemed to sympathize with my tears and confessions of love and loss.

At home in Berkeley, I played with the Ouija board and held seances in the attic. You studied meditation, got a mantra, and began closing your door with a do-not-disturb sign, and I wanted a secret mantra word of my own. You started yoga, and I took the book of postures and tried inverting myself; yoga was fun for bendy legs and little girls. I read tall stacks of books full of fairy tales and myths, and I wanted to become a witch. You didn't mind. I wanted to go to church, and you said I was welcome to but would be going on my own—you were done with it.

You loved your science. You loved rational thought. You loved organ concerts at the Palace of Fine Arts. You loved playing Bach on Sunday mornings. Oddly, you asked to be buried in the family plot. A conventional choice. You are among the Christians of your childhood. I would have imagined cremation and ashes scattered in the sea or in the garden.

Whatever you felt about religion or about God, you were devoted to aesthetics, to natural beauty, to kindness shared with the students you taught, helping them find their way to music, to learning, to exploring a big world. You taught me to be open. I can see your facial expression about church. I think you hated dogma and conformism;

it gave you a sour look to think or talk about it, but you didn't tell me what I could think or do.

> I love you, Mom.
> Kim

Jean, Jerry, and Mom as children.

47

Grape Trays

Dear Mom,

Hard work. This was—and still is—a truism in our family. Way back when, Aunt Jean decided to do some crafting with grape trays. Apparently, they were all the rage in the quasi-antique, craft, folk art world at the time. I was probably about fourteen, so we're talking the early '70s. Aunt Jean asked Grandpa about old grape trays stored at the house. And by house, well, that is another story. A place, a property, a family location. And yes, he had grape trays. The project then turned into one that involved me and involved Meredith. He pulled those grape trays from out back, and they were full of spider webs and dust and dirt. He decided they should be cleaned before he gave them to Jean. I think we were going to drive them to her. He got the broom and assigned Meredith and me to get them in shape for transit.

Standing outside the house, broom in hand, I must have been making a desultory effort, as I am sure I wasn't that into it, and out he came. Grandpa grabbed the broom and started briskly cleaning off the grape tray I was working on. Back and forth, strokes with force, getting that tray into shape, and all the while yelling at me, asking what I was learning, saying I was going to be worthless, telling you that you weren't teaching me the value of hard work, saying I would not succeed and yelling about how I didn't know how to work hard. By the end of the day, my hands had blisters.

Those grape trays go back to actual grape fields. He, and before him his father, grew grapes. Long rows of grapes. There were also almonds and cotton, and at times, wheat and barley. Grapes. You, your brother, and your sister had to pick the grapes in the hot sun of the San Joaquin Valley, pushed to pick, pick, pick, fill your baskets, complete your rows. You were faster than your younger brother and sister, and they still speak of you helping them.

Was my grape tray experience a reenactment of your childhood experience? Work. Work! You have to know how to work hard! Push, push, push, and the promise of punishment. Fierce pummeling if you didn't finish, or even if you did. Violence was never predictable or preventable in our family.

I love you, Mom.
Kim

48

———

Money

Dear Mom,

Money was a super deep subject in our lives. It was central. When we moved to Berkeley, you were single, newly divorced, a mother of two girls, headed to enroll at U.C. Berkeley. Your mother was still alive and very committed to education. She worked and saved up her own money in a separate account, uncontrolled by her husband, and dedicated it to the college education of her children. This was the support you relied on, along with the $300 per month child support my father sent. Our rent was $150 a month in North Berkeley. You made it work.

You bought black spray paint and lacquered fruit crates and plywood to make a Japanese-style dinner table. You put down a big rug and giant pillows in the living room, sawed the legs off a buffet to lower the height, and used steamer trunks for blankets and topped them with plants. You sewed burlap and made Roman shades and stacked more crates for shelves. You took unfinished doors and put them across two drawer cabinets for a big desk and established our home. There was a gigantic stereo and lots of LPs, and we listened to KPFA radio over dinner. We were a part of the revolution. We participated in the Food Conspiracy (for collective buying) and lived communally (periodically). We were hippies. We were down with the man and up with workers' rights. We were anti-establishment, and we were not going to be cogs in the machine. Money was evil. Capitalism was the enemy. We were liberated.

Except we needed money. And your father had some. After Grandma died, we still needed help. So we set up two phones. One for Grandpa to call on, and one for the rest of our lives. 848-7794 was the Grandpa phone. It became my phone in high school. That way, you could have a partner, a man, in the house, and no mistakes would be made by having the wrong person answer the phone. In Grandpa's world, if there was a man in the house, he should provide for you. You were about providing for yourself the best you could, and that included Grandpa's money. We were coached on what to say, or not to say, and over holidays, Malcolm, our stepfather from 1970–1979 (ish), would travel with us to Clovis but stay somewhere else—not with the family. There was a pretense to keep up.

One Christmas, Grandpa put rolled scrolls into cardboard sleeves, wrapped them in colored foil so they looked a bit like the tubes that little Flick candy chocolates used to come in, and gave them out. It was a tally of all the money he ever gave you. When I got older and on my own, I would call Grandpa for help. He would call me a bum. Then he would send a check. When I got sober and independent, I called him, making amends, telling the truth. He asked, "Are you okay now? You're not going to do that anymore? Need any help?" I said yes, I'm okay, and no thank you, I don't need help. He sent me a check. Recently, I learned that Grandpa was truly unable to make a living during the Depression. I thought he had grown up farming with his father and then just carried on. It turns out that he worked as a mechanic and fixed cars. He also invented farm tools. He even left the Valley to go to San Jose and repair cars. Grandma wrote a letter to friends, speaking of their hardship. I am guessing all that talk about being a "bum" stemmed from that time. Perhaps something his father had called him.

After getting sober, I enrolled in college. I struggled to make it through. Sometimes I would say to myself, *Just go to school today. That will be one more day in college before you have to quit and get a job.* Eventually, I turned to you for help. Something I really didn't want to do. You came through with strings. I complied and made it through all the stipulations and through graduation to a first job, when I was able to pay you back. I swore to myself I would not ask you for help again.

In the years that followed, sometimes I experienced being super super super broke. In Philadelphia, I swore that I would not ask you for money. No matter what. I sold my possessions, books, CDs, lamps, computer, camera, whatever I could. I worked with about $20–$30 per week for groceries, learning to spend my way through Trader Joe's, analyzing each dollar for maximum benefit. Friends helped. My friend Rennie's mother collected food for the food bank at her church, and Rennie took me to her house and her mom gave me two bags of groceries. I had a car wreck after a job interview, and my friend Sue paid the deductible. One time, Meredith sent me $50. I persevered for months, almost losing my apartment, until Rennie paid the back rent. No matter what. No matter what. No matter what. I was not calling you for money. I

5/4/75

Dear Kim and Meredith

    I am sorry I missed you Saturday, but I do want to thank you Kim for getting in touch with your mother so that I was able to see her, but the real reason I am writing you is to ask you girls to please help her get through this next month and make things easy for her, along with this please remember you are helping yourselves, since if she doesn't make her degree, it is impossible for her to make enough salary to help you girls go on to school and be anything other than common laborers all the rest of your lives, for I am sure that after you are 18 years old you will get no help from your father and you can both be sure that if you don't change your ways and start studying and not cut classes, I won't help either.

    To me it seems unreal that two good looking smart girls are unable

*A letter to young Kim and Meredith from their grandfather
with his admonishment not to become "bums."*

to figure out the course of life.
either you keep at home and do the
house work and tend to the job of
being good students and good
girls or be bums the rest of your
lives at this time I love you both
very much for else I wouldnt even
write you, please believe me
I or no one else loves bums
please try
   Love Gramp.

was not making it true that I only called you for money. That was your father's story. That was your story. It was not true for me. No matter what.

I found my way through that time. I paid back those who helped me. I had more than $60,000 in debt, and I paid all of that back over the next five years. I struggled. I survived. It was good for me.

You and I never reconciled. Well, not exactly. I wrote you. I loved you. I felt you even though we weren't talking.

Your will was explicit. I was not to ever be empowered with regard to your estate and was left with 15 percent of your assets. I was gracious, knowing that my sister would need those resources. And I was hurt, knowing that you were so intentional about what you were saying with that document.

Even so. I love you, Mom.
Kim

49

Budgets

Dear Mom,

When I finally went to college, I was thirty. One year sober, with some money from your father (he started giving larger cash gifts in the few years before he died, like $5,000), some disability insurance (my trauma and early sobriety were enough to qualify me), some student aid, and some student loans, and I began. The first quarter, I took physics. I got an A in the seminar but a B- in the lab. What a way to start. It's funny to think of it now as I consider your professional career as a scientist. In any case, I made it through about two or more years on a pretty sketchy financial basis. There were weeks when I thought for sure I'd have to quit school and get a full-time job, but somehow, I made it through. I got work-study, I worked temp at a database company, and one of my professors even sat me down and offered to help. The last year, I asked you for help. I tried very much to not ask you for money—that was always tricky, as it involved berating and things like that.

You agreed to help, as a loan, on the condition that I learn budgeting. This involved writing down everything I spent, some kind of budget format, and sharing it with

Mom with one of her many cats.

you. While I resisted this control, I think it left a lasting impression that was helpful—not the control part, but the awareness-of-what-I-spent part. You were amped up at that time about the value of budgeting and felt you hadn't done enough to teach me and Meredith about it— so budgeting it was. I did what was required to have your assistance, and I graduated the next year. I paid you back the year after that from what I earned at my first job. We were even-steven.

Here's what is incredible. In the last seven years of your life, you went through the money earned by you and your brother and sister from the property left by your father and managed by your brother, Jerry, who liquidated the property and distributed the earnings. You began to spend. More than any of us could imagine. No budgeting required.

I've been told you had greater than $7 million US dollars to spend. When you died, you had three homes (all with mortgages), four storage units, a car, several cats, and not much more than $30,000 in the bank. In under ten years, you managed to spend all that money. Could it be somewhere unknown? If only it would reveal itself to the family. Personally, I felt fairly confident you'd spent it. Spent it moment to moment on beautiful things that gave you pleasure. Blown glass, ceramics, and a trompe l'oeil painting in your bathroom. And spent it on relationships that made sense to you, like the next door neighbor and the person who assisted you with odd jobs around the house. And on travel, like to Costa Rica. Somehow, like water through your hands, the money poured and we were all left to wonder how and why you did it.

You left about the same number of years' worth—seven—of unopened mail behind. Stuffed in baskets and boxes, stored underneath the house in the laundry room, hidden under plastic on wooden shelving on your deck, and found below tables with long tablecloths: mountains and piles of paper and mail. There was even a series of neglected and unpaid tax bills. All this postal detritus brought about a lot of consternation and confusion. No one understood how and why that happened. I think I understand now. Even as I thought then that I understood.

I believe you were overwhelmed. And once overwhelmed, you avoided. And once avoiding began, it just got bigger. And so you hid it. You felt like you couldn't handle it. Life is big. Life requires grown-up stuff. All that paper. Too much. No taxes, no budgets, just living, eating, and functioning the best you could. Some people tried to help. Some people seem to have taken advantage—or at the very least, charged you mightily for their time, which was sometimes spent in conversation because it seems you were lonely. And some people who were close to you, like your brother and my sister, just didn't know. I get it. It was too much, too big, too hard. I'm sorry.

I love you, Mom.

Kim

50

———

College

Dear Mom,

Few things had more value in our world than education. In fact, perhaps nothing was deemed more important. Certainly in our household, nothing took precedence over the pursuit of your degree, but that was fueled by a determination to become independent, to survive, to succeed. This fierce dedication to education makes me the third-generation female to complete an advanced college degree education. Grandma, you, me. Incredible. The men—not so much. My father had a high school education. Your father had a middle school education.

This pursuit of education has its roots in your mother's mother. If the family story is true, then the story is that she ironed and mended her way to enough money to get all of her many children (four or five, I believe, although it used to be in my memory as seven or eight) through college. This family folklore may or may not be true. What is true is that your mother had a bachelor's degree in music and she was a concert pianist and a voice teacher. But she was not allowed to perform her talents after she was married. She returned to school for a graduate degree and teaching credential. She became the first person recorded (at least

Kim's Masters graduation from JFK University in June 1996.

in California) to teach independent living skills to the developmentally disabled (called mentally retarded at the time).

How is it that she could be beaten by her husband on a regular basis but emerge undefeated in her efforts to teach human kindness? One thing is for certain: she was equally determined that you and your siblings would have a college education, and she created her own separate funding source for that possibility, just as her mother had before her. She worked. She earned. She saved. And when the time came that you escaped—that really is the word for it—to Berkeley, she was the one on the other end of the phone, providing you with money to survive, to make it, to take your little girls, to enroll in college, and to succeed. Education. You were firmly committed to it. You supported my completion of college and my sister's completion of college, and you were equally dedicated to supporting your grandchildren's opportunity to advance. Even in the last years before you died, you were advocating, pushing, really, for them to get outside college prep tutoring, work hard, go to school, and advance.

This, if anything, is our family creed.

I love you, Mom.

Kim

51

—

Shopping Trip

Dear Mom,

One time in your fifties, you decided you wanted a new wardrobe. Probably because you'd been working out with a trainer. You were a professor by then, and your standard wardrobe consisted of jeans, turtleneck, down vest, and tennies or hiking boots. Perhaps it was because you began presenting papers at conferences. Or maybe it just seemed like a good idea.

The super amazing thing was that you wanted me to help you shop. I think we went to I. Magnin's—fancy. I always loved fashion, and it was a source of ridicule from you to me when I was younger. In my teens and young adulthood, I worked in retail and pretty much focused on two goals: fashion and being able to dance salsa with any partner on any floor. That was about as much as I could focus on. Which, of course, is part of why you concluded I was a waste of a good brain.

But this day, this experience, this moment, you needed me. You wanted my help. You saw me. You wanted to share with me. We were on an adventure. A shopping trip. You and me. It was a generous act on your part to ask for my help.

I ran back and forth to the dressing room, pulling sizes, matching looks, showing you how outfits could be put together. It was incredible. You looked great, and I was happy to find pretty things for you. You spent $5,000 on clothes that day. That was more money than I could possibly imagine ever spending on clothes. It blew my mind. And it made me super happy. The clothes were beautiful, and I had helped you find them.

I love you, Mom.
Kim

52

—

Body

Dear Mom,

I just did a photo shoot a week ago and got the first set of pictures back. I am all boobs, belly, and butt. Although proud of my ass, I am equally ashamed of the rest of my curves, so maternal, so round, so full. When you were in your fifties, you started working out with a trainer. You shared with me that it gave you a feeling of power, that you would look at yourself in the mirror, working with the weights, and see yourself as a warrior. I don't know what happened because that phase passed and you steadily gained weight. I don't know how much at first because I have a totally fucked up and skewed weirdness about weight. Mine. And yours.

When you stopped being beautiful, which is to say when your face was twisted with anger and your body filled out and you and I were at war with each other (and perhaps it was just the normal maturation of age, and maybe you weren't even that big, and for some reason, I resented this change of maturity in you), well, I felt oddly reviled. And ashamed. On your behalf and of my feelings.

And now, today, I work with a trainer, and I have a belly, and when I opened the file of photos, what leapt

Kim Cook; photo by Kerry Kehoe.

out at me from the computer screen was all that curvature and softness, and I could barely see the light in my eye. I'm pretty sure I missed a lot of stuff about you. I am told you sat in your room near a small refrigerator that was filled with candy, and you became more than a hundred pounds overweight. Lying dead in the hospital, you were all flat softness in a hospital gown. This thing about body image is some trivial and powerful shit.

I love you, Mom.
Kim

53

Leaving

Dear Mom,

Today is the day of shift. It is the day before the last day before I take a long trip. I am taking leave from home. I am unstable, emotional, grumpy, and prone to tears.

Preparing to leave always shakes me. I have trouble forming emotions that use words like *excited, opportunity, possibility, good fortune,* and *adventure.* Instead, the words that arise within me on waves of feelings are *leaving home, being sent away, distress,* and *rupture.*

This rising tide swirls around my heart and pulls me under with memory cords that include the last of many occasions when I was sent away from home. This was in 1975, when you sat down with me and Meredith and said basically this:

"I have come to understand that I cannot be both a good scientist and a good mother. I believe I can be a good scientist. I am accepting that I am not equipped to be a mother. I've decided that the two of you will go to boarding school. My father will help pay for it. You can pick anywhere you like. You cannot go to the same place."

Holy fuck.

Your reasoning for why Meredith and I could not stay together was your conviction that I was a bad influence on her. You seemed to have assigned us roles from infancy. Me bad. Her good. It was heartbreaking for us to be sent away. It was not the first time.

When you died, I had this amazing moment of seeing clearly the way in which Meredith and I were viewed and cultivated. Meredith not intelligent, dependent, stay at home = Good. Me intelligent, independent, leave home = Bad. These assignments were actually your interpretation of yourself. If you stayed home and didn't go to college and needed your husband and your father, you were good. When you made the break to go to Berkeley, you became independent and bad.

This simple equation made sense to me all of a sudden. You were merged with us, we were you, and you split us along the lines of the division inside of you. Until you couldn't figure it out anymore, and then we were sent away.

And now, all these years later, going out into the world still breaks my heart. Every time.

I love you, Mom.
Kim

Garden

Dear Mom,

A couple of weeks ago, I came back from a long time away: five weeks in Montreal and New York. The surprise discovery was a fully grown cauliflower in my garden. I had planted a garden last spring that turned out indifferently. It seemed that many local birds and squirrels were feasting on the tasty green shoots whenever they emerged, and not much made it to fruition. Then, suddenly, I come back home and here is this luscious curtain of green leaves surrounding a round head of cauliflower. It was a bouquet of a single head, a welcome and fortuitous sign. My yellow rose was also poised to blossom, the lemons were hard and partly green but on their way, the chard was burgeoning, and the camellias were beginning to fade from their mid-winter glory in red and pink.

My houseplants are coming along, although the coleus isn't quite finding the place it wants to be and the orchid is dwindling, but in general, all is well with the botanical things I am growing. I cut back the monkey flowers, took the weeds out of the bamboo pot, and gave the bougainvillea an extra bit of soil nurturing and water. Taking care. Tending the plants. Enjoying their growth, their life, their beauty.

This is one of the gifts of you. You are why I know words like hydrangea and fuchsia. In Clovis, where we began, there were fig trees (you loved eating figs the rest of your life) and gardenia plants, azaleas and rhododendrons; your mother loved her garden as well.

When we moved to Berkeley, you hung Boston ferns in the windows, put palm trees around the living room, and organized a work party to plant the little patch of dirt outside our duplex. You hung an orchid plant that grew and grew, blossoming outside our front door for more than a decade. The Monterey cypress, the birch trees, and the eucalyptus, that you planted in that little patch of dirt, grew tall and strong and are still there. The plants small and large that rested in that garden gave peace and beauty to that space.

When you bought your home in Davenport, your sense of garden stretched and expanded to include two decks, floating stairs, a stone path, small fountains, sculptures, and citrus trees in big Italian planters. You had bird feeders and wind chimes and hand-cast bells hanging from trees. Your vision kept growing and evolving and flowering with ideas of beauty and a sense of a dreamlike place. It was a marvel. A wonderland. A mystical journey. A poem.

There was magic in you. I feel that magic in my garden.

I love you, Mom.

Kim

55

The Force Umbilical

Dear Mom,

In the end, it turns out you are always with me. This afternoon as the light fades and the fog rolls in, I remember how much you loved the fog. My wind chimes are melodic and reminiscent of your home at the beach. I travel, and I am aware of how you gave me access to a bigger world. I make my eggs in the morning, and the pepper is a reminder of how you loved pepper on your eggs. I can see your hands and your love of handmade jewelry; semi-precious stones were always more interesting to you than diamonds.

I've been afraid that we might be locked in battle, falling through space and time like two warriors who will never complete their karmic destiny. That I will never be rid of the struggle with you, never free of the pain of loving you. That could be true.

When you died, the sensation I had was of the force umbilical. I am connected to you forever, and the force of the umbilical cord is one of forever linkage. The pain of losing you is a jagged knife that runs the length of my body, throat to belly, ripping me open and tearing out my heart. I lay on the floor at my friend's house, unable to absorb the truth of your death, tears leaking out of the

Mom and Kim.

sides of my eyes as I stared out the window at the gentle currents on the water. The moon rose at night, and still I lay there. Immobile.

You are my constant. I am made of you. Many times, I tried to talk to you about our story. You couldn't hold it. The denial would come rippling up and out of you like a snake unfurling, and you would strike with so much venom it would cause me to fall to my knees, a sensation of the floor dropping out from under me. I had no idea how to address it. I wanted us to be open and reconciled. When I learned more about trauma and the likelihood that you had borderline personality disorder, I learned that it is possible that your history made it such that you did not remember the things you did to me. That your protestations that I was making things up, that you never beat me, that you did not know why I would tell such lies about you, were what you truly believed to be true. That was a cruel blow to me, the idea that I made you suffer in my quest to have truth between us about my suffering and our family history of suffering. Incomprehensible. Tragic.

When you were ill, my sister tells me she had a conversation with you and you said something about everyone having a little girl inside. Mom, you were so fragile. You were so tough.

I don't know how to experience this way in which you are both gone and present. I don't know how to hold my vulnerability alongside my resilience. I don't know how to let go of pain and receive joy. There is so much sorrow.

I am loved. Thankfully. Unbelievably, I survived. I love. You.

I love you,
Kim

Postscript

When I finally went to college at thirty years old, I gained the benefit of being able to take classes that would directly apply to the life I had lived and the things I needed to learn. One of those classes was called, "My Life and Development." In that class, we learned the concept of the *good enough mother*. I am not going to pretend to offer the research or even to say that my takeaway is accurate. What I can say is that I understood from this class the idea of the *good enough mother* is that we come to terms with the ways in which our parents, or even our lives, can disappoint us. And then we let them be *good enough.*

How does this come about? How did it come about for me? Many paths of learning over the years have led to my ability to hold the paradox of the good and not good that coexisted in my mother. My mother was particularly averse to the sensation of having needs, whether her own or her response to the needs of another. The expectation was often that I keep my needs from interfering with her life. However, she also provided me with many, many experiences, and she met my basic needs for food and shelter as she struggled through her own life processes.

I've learned that no one person can, or likely will, provide us with all that we need. One clear element of healing for me was the love and nurturing of others. So many people, particularly women friends, professional therapists, bodyworkers, and movement teachers, contributed to my growth. I am eternally grateful for their generosity and grace that have not only enhanced but actually saved my life.

In therapy, I came to learn many truths, two of which I will share here. The first is that a lack of empathy for myself (and absent from my childhood) was harmful. I had to own, hold, and share the truth of my experience and find compassion for myself. This ability to have compassion for myself has given me the gift of compassion for others, including my family. The other truth is to beware of idealizing people and future possibilities. My mother often lived in a world of memory and future promises, all made softer and prettier through the lens of idealized fantasies. This translated for me into expectations of myself and others that are unrealistic and ultimately unkind. This is where the *good enough* concept serves me.

Life unfolds. I am not the movie star or Rhodes Scholar I might have expected of myself. However, I am *good enough.*

Thank you, reader.

I love you,
Kim

Acknowledgments

Gratitude is more than a notion; it is a living act, a conscious choice, a way to retrieve oneself in the midst of struggle. Find gratitude and you can find a way forward. For me to express gratitude in a full way would take many pages, so I say globally: I am grateful. I have been aided and helped and taught and comforted and guided and loved by so many people. I start by thanking my dear friend Rennie and my sister Meredith. In 2001, Rennie said, "Kim, reassuring you that I love you is exhausting." I was still learning to live in a way that could receive love. In 2023, when I had cancer, Meredith said, "I am trying to figure out how I can help you." And finally, I understood that when people want to love me, I can let them. I am safe. It is safe to be loved.

Once upon a time, the people who loved me also hurt me. I love them back now through this book of letters to my mother. It is never too late to reconcile because reconciliation can live in your heart even if you cannot achieve it with another. That is difficult to accept. Years ago, when a job I had went bad, I learned to say to myself, "Some situations have factors over which you have no control." Now I would probably say that is true in all situations! We do have the ability to choose what we say to ourselves about what happened, to learn, to grow, to expand our hearts, and to move forward. As they say in recovery, "simple but not easy."

With that, I thank my friend Amy, who taught me something about what "normal" is and who always tells me she loves me unconditionally. To my therapist Diane, who taught me the value of self-empathy. To my sister, Meredith, who exemplifies kindness and goodness. To my friend Rennie, who gave me so much, including a greater ability to value myself. To Jeffrey, who is so fun to spark creative thought with. To Anna and Jim, who set an example of the road ahead and who provide me with so much joy and inspiration. Thank you also to Sarah, who embodies grace and sass and is the very real deal, and to Suhaila, who captured my heart long ago. The circle is big and includes my Philadelphia and DC Folks, Phil, Anna, and Michelle, who loved me through some super hard times, and my LA Peeps like Jess, my New Orleans Family, Joycelyn, Asante, Lindsay, Arthur, Dan, and Neil, and while we are down south, my Austin friends Marjory, the best Sunday School teacher ever, Nick, and Heidi. In New York, Monique, in Barcelona, Marta, in Black Rock City, Brody, Megan, and Gloria. And here in San Luis Obispo, Dr. Michelle at Zen Den, Brian Baird Builders, Lucia, Ryan, Josh at Mint, Danielle,Taryn, Gizmo, and dog Ollie. Many many many people helped me save my life.

Thank you to my editor, Jennifer Jas, and the remarkable book designer, Carla Green. Thank you to my early readers for your time and encouragement. Finally, thank you to my family—you gave me a start and did the best you could. I love you.

Book Group Discussion Guide

1. The author suggests that the pain in families is intergenerational. Do you think that suffering is partly passed down through families? How might this begin to change?

2. Today, the topic of gender is much more present in conversation. What do you think about this as a potentially feminist issue?

3. Do you have examples like the author's mother where a woman in science or another career was disregarded because of being a woman?

4. Freedom from a small town and getting an education are themes in this book. Are rural towns still places with less access to advanced education? How might children raised in rural areas have increased opportunities where they are? Has the internet changed this?

5. Alcohol and drugs also make an appearance in this book. Do you see a connection between family violence and substance abuse? Is it reasonable to think of this as an illness? How might there be more social support to address substance abuse?

6. Do you believe that the phrase "hurt people, hurt people" makes sense? How do you personally address the ideas of compassion and forgiveness in your life?

7. Music, beauty, plants, art, and reading books all form a backdrop in this book. How important do you think these elements are to daily life?

8. What is your particular form of Sunday morning ritual? Church, cleaning house, concerts in the park?

9. What is your favorite memory with your mother or an adult woman in your life?

10. What are your favorite books? The author mentions mystery novelists Sue Grafton and Louise Penny; do you like books like that? Which authors?

11. Did you have teachers or mentors as a young person? How did they influence you and the person you became?

Book Group Discussion Guide
with Bereavement Questions

1. How might you feel if you lost a loved one and were not reconciled? Has this happened to you or someone you know?
2. Might you have experienced unfinished matters with someone who passed, even though you were in contact?
3. Can we process through our losses alone? What kind of support might be useful or important—even critical?
4. Is it possible to accept death as a part of life? How are you thinking about the time when your own passing occurs?
5. Do you feel like, as a society, we are able to talk about and feel comfortable with death? Since society is not universally the same, how is it where you live? Do you know of other places where it is different?
6. After a person is gone, how might you still feel connected to them? Is it possible to release old hurts and resentments with love?
7. Can you imagine how you want to be thought of when you are gone?
8. Are you doing anything in particular to leave a legacy?

9. They say you can't take it with you. Do you think anything does live on once you've died?
10. The author titled the book *What Remains Is Love*. Can love be left behind or taken with us once we are gone?

Recommended Reading List

*The Courage to Heal: A Guide for Women Survivors
of Child Sexual Abuse*
Ellen Bass and Laura Davis

*Understanding the Borderline Mother: Helping Her
Children Transcend the Intense, Unpredictable, and
Volatile Relationship*
Christine Ann Lawson

*Surviving a Borderline Parent: How to Heal Your
Childhood Wounds and Build Trust, Boundaries,
and Self-Esteem*
Kimberlee Roth and Freda B. Friedman, PhD, LCSW

*Trauma and Recovery: The Aftermath of Violence—from
Domestic Abuse to Political Terror*
Judith Herman, MD

When Things Fall Apart: Heart Advice for Difficult Times
Pema Chodron

The Big Book of Alcoholics Anonymous
AA World Services, Inc.

Twelve Steps and Twelve Traditions
AA World Services, Inc.

About the Author

Kim Cook creates: Impact. Stories. Community projects. Places. Experiences. Spectacle. Known for her ability to take conceptual work and translate it into results, Kim has established herself as a trusted collaborator and ally with a multitude of artists and organizations.

Kim's professional background includes leading Creative Initiatives for Burning Man, working as a Creative Director for Montreal's Moment Factory, and founding New Orleans' LUNA Fête Festival when she served as the CEO for the Arts Council New Orleans. She is also the force behind the creation of a podcast series and curriculum on Cultural Synergy with the United States Institute of Peace. She has a B.A. in Performing Arts, an M.A. in Arts and Consciousness, and a certificate in Circus Dramaturgie from the French and Belgian National Circus Schools. Kim is a nine-time National Endowment for the Arts grant recipient and a Kennedy Center for the Performing Arts Fellow.

Her creative work includes theater, circus, dance, festivals, visual art installations, place shaping, digital media, social/virtual reality, NFT production, spoken word, and writing. She successfully builds urban, regional, national, and international projects that are dynamic, and sometimes she does things for the adventure, the learning, the discovery, the fun.

www.kimcookcreates.com

www.ingramcontent.com/pod-product-compliance
Lightning Source LLC
Chambersburg PA
CBHW021525150726
47990CB00006B/2099